Smoothie Recipe Book

Quick and Easy Blends for Any Time of Day – Family-Friendly and Illustrated

Rachel Terry

Copyright

This book is copyright © 2024 by Rachel Terry. All rights are reserved. Any unauthorized reproduction, sharing, or distribution of this work, in part or in its entirety, is strictly prohibited. This includes any form of digital or analog replica, such as photocopying, recording, or information storage and retrieval systems, except as permitted under sections of copyright law for brief quotations in a review.

Legal Disclaimer

The material presented in this book is intended for informational purposes only. No warranty, express or implied, on the quality, precision, or suitability for a particular purpose of the content is offered. The author shall not be held responsible for any direct, consequential, or incidental damages arising from using or misusing any information herein. While every effort has been made to ensure the accuracy of the material in this book, neither the author nor the publisher accepts responsibility for any mistakes, inaccuracies, or omissions. If you need professional advice, please consult a qualified professional.

Your purchase and use of this book indicate your acceptance of these terms and conditions.

Table of Content

Introduction 5
What is a Smoothie? 6
The Health Benefits of Smoothies 7
Importance of Using Fresh Ingredients 9
Tips for Making Smoothies (Equipment, Techniques, etc.) 11
Breakfast Blends 13
    Morning Berry Awakening 14
    Oats & Cinnamon Start 15
    Peachy Keen Sunrise 16
    Banana Nut Morning 17
    Apple Pie Energizer 18
    Tangy Orange Daybreak 19
    Cherry Almond Boost 20
    Avocado Toast Smoothie 21
Seasonal Smoothies 22
    Spring Melon Medley 23
    Summer Berry Splash 24
    Autumn Pumpkin Patch Smoothie 25
    Winter Citrus Zest Fondue 26
    Harvest Apple Cinnamon Swirl 27
    Tropical Mango Rapture 28
    Cozy Pear Ginger Blend 29
    Berry Cherry Jubilee Smoothie 30
Kid-Friendly Creations 31
    Strawberry Banana Smile 32
    Peanut Butter Jelly Time 33
    Hidden Veggie Chocolate Surprise 34
    Apple Orchard Adventure 35
    Tropical Treasure Hunt 36
    Purple Berry Galaxy 37

    Green Monster Mystery 38
    Orange Creamsicle Delight 39
Diabetic-Friendly Smoothies 40
    Low-Sugar Berry Bliss 41
    Cinnamon Apple Balance 42
    Creamy Avocado Dream 43
    Ginger Peach Soothe 44
    Tangy Raspberry Refresh 45
    Kale and Blueberry Burst 46
    Chia Seed Citrus Fusion 47
    Coco-Cucumber Cooler 48
Detox Smoothie 49
    Lemon Ginger Zest 50
    Apple Cider Vinegar Revive 51
    Cucumber Mint Refresher 52
    Carrot Citrus Purge 53
    Simple Spinach Detox 54
    Celery Apple Cleanse 55
    Pineapple Parsley Pep 56
    Watermelon Basil Bliss 57
Smoothies for Weight Loss 58
    Berry Metabolism Booster 59
    Citrus Slimmer 60
    Kale and Apple Shred Smoothie 61
    Banana Oat Balance 62
    Cinnamon Almond Swirl 63
    Grapefruit and Spinach Trim 64
    Carrot and Orange Essence 65
    Green Tea Infusion 66
Green Veggie Blends 67
    Spinach Sunshine Sip 68

- Kale Kickstart Fusion 69
- Celery Zing Twist 70
- Garden Greens Smoothie 71
- Peppy Parsley Potion 72
- Crisp Cucumber Cooler 73
- Basil & Spinach Refresher 74
- Romaine Calm & Blend On 75

Post-Workout Power Blends 76
- Protein Power-Up 77
- Banana-Peanut Punch 78
- Muscle Recovery Mix 79
- Berry Blast Recharge 80
- Choco-Nut Energy Boost 81
- Tropical Refuel Shake 82
- Sweet Spinach Stamina 83
- Almond-Date Dynamo 84

Conclusion 85

Index 86

Introduction

Welcome to the "Smoothie Recipe Book," your ultimate guide to crafting delicious and nutritious smoothies at home. Whether you're a smoothie enthusiast or just beginning your journey into the world of blended beverages, this book offers a wide array of recipes and tips to help you make the most of every smoothie.

In today's fast-paced world, maintaining a healthy diet can be challenging. Smoothies provide a quick, convenient, and enjoyable way to ensure you're getting the essential nutrients your body needs. They are incredibly versatile, customizable, and perfect for any time of day – whether you need a quick breakfast, a post-workout boost, or a refreshing snack.

This book is much more than a collection of recipes; it's a comprehensive guide to understanding the art and science of smoothie making. We'll begin by exploring what a smoothie is and the various types you can create. You'll learn about the incredible health benefits of incorporating smoothies into your diet, from boosting your immune system to enhancing your energy levels. We'll also emphasize the importance of using fresh, high-quality ingredients to ensure you get the best flavor and nutritional value from every sip.

To help you get started, we've included a section on essential equipment and techniques, providing you with the knowledge you need to blend like a pro. From choosing the right blender to mastering the perfect consistency, these tips will ensure your smoothie-making experience is both enjoyable and successful.

The chapters ahead are organized to cater to different needs and preferences. Whether you're looking to detox, lose weight, boost your post-workout recovery, or create kid-friendly and diabetic-friendly options, you'll find a wealth of recipes designed to support your health goals.

So, grab your blender and get ready to embark on a delicious journey to better health. With this book in hand, you'll discover that making nutritious and tasty smoothies is not only easy but also incredibly rewarding. Let's blend our way to a healthier, happier you!

What is a Smoothie?

A smoothie is a thick, creamy beverage made by blending a variety of ingredients, primarily fruits and vegetables, with a liquid base. What makes smoothies unique is their versatility and the endless combinations of flavors and nutrients you can create to suit your taste preferences and dietary needs.

At its core, a smoothie typically includes the following components:
- **Base Liquid:** This is the liquid that helps blend all the ingredients together, giving the smoothie its desired consistency. Common base liquids include water, milk (dairy or plant-based), juice, coconut water, and yogurt.
- **Fruits and Vegetables:** These are the stars of any smoothie, providing the bulk of the flavor, nutrients, and natural sweetness. Popular fruits include bananas, berries, mangoes, and apples, while common vegetables include spinach, kale, cucumbers, and carrots.
- **Add-ins and Enhancers:** These ingredients boost the nutritional profile and flavor of your smoothie. They can include protein powders, seeds (like chia or flaxseeds), nuts, spices (like cinnamon or turmeric), sweeteners (like honey or maple syrup), and superfoods (like spirulina or acai).

Smoothies can be classified into several types based on their primary ingredients and intended purpose:
- **Fruit Smoothies:** These are the most common type, featuring a blend of various fruits and a liquid base. They are naturally sweet and packed with vitamins, minerals, and antioxidants.
- **Green Smoothies:** These include a mix of leafy greens and other vegetables, often combined with fruits to balance the flavor. Green smoothies are known for their detoxifying and nutrient-dense properties.
- **Protein Smoothies:** These are designed to support muscle recovery and growth, often incorporating protein-rich ingredients like protein powders, Greek yogurt, nuts, and seeds.
- **Meal Replacement Smoothies:** These are more substantial, containing a balance of carbohydrates, proteins, and fats to serve as a complete meal. They often include ingredients like oats, nut butters, and avocados for added satiety.

Whether you're looking to enhance your diet with more fruits and vegetables, support your fitness goals, or simply enjoy a delicious and refreshing drink, smoothies offer a versatile and enjoyable way to nourish your body. With the right ingredients and a bit of creativity, you can blend up endless combinations that cater to your personal health goals and taste preferences.

The Health Benefits of Smoothies

Smoothies are much more than just a delicious treat; they are a powerhouse of nutrition, offering numerous health benefits that can support your overall well-being. By incorporating a variety of fruits, vegetables, and other nutritious ingredients, smoothies can provide a convenient and effective way to improve your diet and health. Here are some of the key health benefits of including smoothies in your daily routine:

1. Nutrient Density
Smoothies are packed with essential vitamins, minerals, and antioxidants that are crucial for maintaining good health. By blending a variety of fruits and vegetables, you can create a nutrient-dense drink that provides a significant portion of your daily nutritional requirements. This can help you meet your dietary needs, especially if you have a busy lifestyle or struggle to consume enough whole fruits and vegetables.

2. Improved Digestion
Many smoothie ingredients are rich in dietary fiber, which is essential for healthy digestion. Fiber helps regulate bowel movements, prevent constipation, and promote a healthy gut microbiome. Smoothies that include fibrous fruits, vegetables, and seeds can contribute to better digestive health and overall gut function.

3. Enhanced Energy Levels
Smoothies can be an excellent source of natural energy. The carbohydrates from fruits and the proteins and healthy fats from add-ins like nuts, seeds, and yogurt provide a balanced energy boost that can help you stay energized throughout the day. Unlike sugary snacks and drinks, smoothies offer sustained energy without the crash.

4. Weight Management
Incorporating smoothies into your diet can support weight management efforts. When made with the right ingredients, smoothies can be filling and satisfying, helping to curb hunger and reduce unhealthy snacking. By choosing low-calorie, nutrient-dense ingredients, you can enjoy a delicious smoothie that supports your weight loss or maintenance goals.

5. Immune System Support
Smoothies can be fortified with ingredients that boost your immune system. Fruits like citrus, berries, and kiwi are rich in vitamin C, while leafy greens like spinach and kale provide essential nutrients like vitamin A and iron. Adding superfoods like ginger, turmeric, and spirulina can further enhance the immune-boosting properties of your smoothies.

6. Detoxification
Certain smoothie ingredients have natural detoxifying properties. Green smoothies, in particular, are known for their ability to cleanse the body and support liver function. Ingredients like leafy greens, cucumber, and lemon help flush out toxins and promote overall detoxification.

7. Hydration
Smoothies can contribute to your daily hydration needs, especially when made with high-water-content fruits and vegetables, such as watermelon, cucumber, and strawberries. Staying

hydrated is essential for overall health, as it supports bodily functions, improves skin health, and aids in digestion.

8. Improved Skin Health
The vitamins and antioxidants found in many smoothie ingredients can promote healthy, glowing skin. Vitamins A and C, found in fruits like mango and oranges, help reduce inflammation and promote collagen production. Additionally, the hydration provided by smoothies can help keep your skin moisturized and radiant.

9. Better Mental Health
The nutrients in smoothies can also benefit your mental health. Omega-3 fatty acids from ingredients like flaxseeds and chia seeds support brain health, while the antioxidants in berries can help protect the brain from oxidative stress. The natural sugars in fruits provide an immediate energy boost that can improve mood and cognitive function.

10. Customizable Nutrition
One of the greatest benefits of smoothies is their versatility. You can tailor your smoothie to meet your specific nutritional needs and preferences. Whether you need a post-workout recovery drink, a meal replacement, or a quick snack, you can customize your smoothie with the right ingredients to achieve your health goals.

Incorporating smoothies into your daily routine is an easy and delicious way to enhance your overall health. With the right combination of ingredients, you can enjoy a variety of health benefits that support your body and mind. So, grab your blender and start reaping the rewards of this nutritious and convenient beverage.

Importance of Using Fresh Ingredients

When it comes to making smoothies, the quality of your ingredients can significantly impact the taste, nutritional value, and overall experience of your beverage. Using fresh ingredients is crucial for creating smoothies that are not only delicious but also packed with essential nutrients. Here are several reasons why fresh ingredients are so important in smoothie making:

1. Superior Flavor
Fresh ingredients bring out the best flavors in your smoothies. Fruits and vegetables at their peak ripeness have the most vibrant and rich tastes, which can make your smoothie more enjoyable. Fresh ingredients can transform a simple smoothie into a flavorful and satisfying treat, encouraging you to consume more nutrient-dense foods.

2. Higher Nutritional Value
Fresh fruits and vegetables retain their full spectrum of vitamins, minerals, and antioxidants, which can degrade over time after harvesting. By using fresh ingredients, you ensure that you are getting the maximum nutritional benefit from your smoothie. This can help you meet your daily nutrient requirements more effectively, supporting your overall health and well-being.

3. Better Texture
Fresh ingredients contribute to a smoother and more appealing texture in your smoothies. Overripe or stale fruits and vegetables can lead to a mushy or uneven consistency, which can be off-putting. Fresh produce, on the other hand, blends more easily and uniformly, resulting in a creamy and consistent texture.

4. Enhanced Freshness and Vitality
Using fresh ingredients in your smoothies adds a level of freshness and vitality that processed or frozen ingredients often lack. This can make your smoothies more refreshing and invigorating, especially when consumed right after blending. The natural, vibrant colors of fresh produce also make your smoothies visually appealing and appetizing.

5. Fewer Preservatives and Additives
Fresh ingredients are free from the preservatives and additives often found in processed or pre-packaged foods. This means your smoothies are more natural and healthier. By choosing fresh produce, you can avoid unnecessary chemicals and enjoy a cleaner, more wholesome beverage.

6. Support for Local Farmers and Sustainable Practices
Using fresh, locally sourced ingredients supports local farmers and sustainable agricultural practices. By purchasing seasonal produce from local markets, you help reduce the carbon footprint associated with transporting food over long distances. This not only benefits the environment but also ensures you have access to the freshest, most flavorful ingredients available.

7. Seasonal Variety
Fresh ingredients allow you to take advantage of the best produce each season has to offer. Seasonal fruits and vegetables are often at their peak flavor and nutritional value, providing a

delicious and diverse range of ingredients for your smoothies. Incorporating seasonal produce into your smoothies can keep your recipes exciting and varied throughout the year.

8. Better Health Outcomes
Consuming fresh ingredients in your smoothies can lead to better health outcomes. Fresh produce is typically lower in calories and higher in essential nutrients compared to processed alternatives. This can support weight management, improve digestion, boost immunity, and enhance overall health.

9. Improved Hydration
Fresh fruits and vegetables have high water content, which can contribute to your daily hydration needs. Proper hydration is essential for maintaining energy levels, supporting cognitive function, and promoting overall health. Fresh ingredients help ensure your smoothies are hydrating and revitalizing.

10. Greater Control Over Ingredients
Using fresh ingredients gives you greater control over what goes into your smoothies. You can select organic produce, avoid allergens, and tailor your smoothies to meet your specific dietary preferences and health goals. This level of control allows you to create personalized smoothies that are both delicious and nutritious.

In conclusion, using fresh ingredients is key to making the most out of your smoothie experience. Not only do fresh fruits and vegetables enhance the flavor and texture of your smoothies, but they also provide superior nutritional benefits and support a healthier lifestyle. So, next time you prepare a smoothie, reach for the freshest ingredients available to enjoy a truly delightful and nourishing drink.

Tips for Making Smoothies (Equipment, Techniques, etc.)

Creating the perfect smoothie involves more than just throwing ingredients into a blender. By using the right equipment, mastering essential techniques, and following some key tips, you can elevate your smoothie-making game and enjoy consistently delicious and nutritious beverages. Here are some tips to help you make the best smoothies:

1. Choose the Right Blender
The foundation of a great smoothie is a high-quality blender. Here are some features to look for:
- **Power**: A powerful blender (at least 500 watts) can handle tough ingredients like ice, frozen fruit, and fibrous vegetables.
- **Blade Design**: Sharp, durable blades ensure a smooth blend. Some blenders have specialized blades for crushing ice or pureeing fruits and vegetables.
- **Capacity**: Consider the size of the blender jar. A larger jar is useful for making multiple servings, while a smaller, personal-sized blender is ideal for single servings.
- **Ease of Cleaning**: Choose a blender with removable, dishwasher-safe parts for easy cleaning.

2. Use Fresh and High-Quality Ingredients
For the best flavor and nutritional value, use fresh, high-quality ingredients:
- **Fruits and Vegetables**: Opt for ripe, seasonal produce. Wash and prepare them properly before blending.
- **Liquid Base**: Choose a healthy liquid base such as water, milk (dairy or plant-based), coconut water, or fresh juice.
- **Add-ins**: Enhance your smoothies with nutrient-rich add-ins like chia seeds, flaxseeds, protein powder, nut butters, and superfoods.

3. Master the Art of Blending
Follow these blending tips for a smooth and consistent texture:
- **Layering**: Layer your ingredients in the blender starting with the liquid base, followed by soft ingredients (yogurt, nut butter), then leafy greens, fruits, and finally, ice or frozen items. This helps the blades work efficiently.
- **Blending Time**: Blend on a low setting to start, then gradually increase to high. Blend until smooth, usually for about 30-60 seconds.
- **Pulse Function**: Use the pulse function to break down larger chunks and to mix in ingredients that might stick to the sides of the blender.

4. Balance Your Ingredients
Create a balanced smoothie by including a variety of ingredients:
- **Carbohydrates**: Fruits provide natural sugars and energy.
- **Proteins**: Greek yogurt, protein powder, and nut butters add protein for muscle repair and satiety.
- **Fats**: Avocados, nuts, and seeds contribute healthy fats that keep you full and support nutrient absorption.
- **Fiber**: Leafy greens, oats, and chia seeds add fiber for digestive health.

5. Experiment with Flavors and Textures
Keep your smoothies interesting by experimenting with different flavors and textures:
- **Spices and Herbs**: Add a pinch of cinnamon, nutmeg, or fresh mint for extra flavor.
- **Sweeteners**: If needed, use natural sweeteners like honey, maple syrup, or dates.
- **Textures**: Add a handful of nuts, seeds, or granola on top for a crunchy texture.

6. Prepping and Storing Ingredients
Save time by prepping ingredients in advance:
- **Freezing**: Freeze fruits and vegetables in portions for quick use. Pre-chop and freeze them in freezer bags.
- **Pre-measuring**: Measure out add-ins like seeds, powders, and nuts in advance and store them in small containers.

7. Adjust Consistency
Adjust the consistency of your smoothie to your liking:
- **Thicker Smoothies**: Use less liquid and more frozen ingredients or add a spoonful of Greek yogurt or avocado.
- **Thinner Smoothies**: Add more liquid (water, milk, juice) until you reach the desired consistency.

8. Clean Your Blender Properly
Cleaning your blender immediately after use prevents residue from sticking and makes the process easier:
- **Quick Clean**: Fill the blender halfway with warm water and a drop of dish soap. Blend on high for 30 seconds, then rinse thoroughly.
- **Deep Clean**: For a more thorough clean, disassemble the blender and wash all parts in warm, soapy water or place them in the dishwasher if they are dishwasher-safe.

9. Pay Attention to Portion Sizes
Smoothies can be high in calories if not portioned properly:
- **Measure Ingredients**: Be mindful of the quantity of high-calorie ingredients like nuts, seeds, and sweeteners.
- **Serving Size**: Aim for a serving size that fits your nutritional needs, usually around 8-12 ounces for a snack and 16-20 ounces for a meal replacement.

10. Enjoy Fresh
Smoothies are best enjoyed fresh to maximize their flavor and nutritional benefits. If you need to store a smoothie, keep it in an airtight container in the refrigerator for up to 24 hours, and shake or stir before drinking.

By following these tips and techniques, you can create smoothies that are not only tasty but also packed with nutrition. Whether you're looking for a quick breakfast, a post-workout recovery drink, or a refreshing snack, mastering the art of smoothie making can help you enjoy a healthy and delicious beverage anytime.

Breakfast Blends

Morning Berry Awakening

Start your day with the energizing zest of mixed berries in this luscious Morning Berry Awakening smoothie. A blend of sweet and tart flavors makes this drink irresistible, while the generous dose of nutrients prepares you for an active day ahead.

Equipment:

Blender, Measuring cups, Glasses

Ingredients:

- One cup of assorted frozen berries, including blackberries, raspberries, blueberries, and strawberries
- 1 banana, sliced
- 3/4 cup Greek yogurt, plain
- 1/2 cup orange juice, freshly squeezed
- 1/4 cup rolled oats
- 1 tablespoon honey (or to taste)
- A handful of fresh spinach (optional for added nutrients)

Tips:

Consider adding a scoop of your preferred vanilla protein powder for an additional protein boost. To make this smoothie even more refreshing, blend with a few ice cubes or chill your serving glasses beforehand.

Nutritional Information:

Calories: 235, Protein: 11g, Carbohydrates: 42g, Fat: 3g, Fiber: 6g, Cholesterol: 8 mg, Sodium: 31 mg, Potassium: 523 mg

2 SERVINGS **5 MINUTES**

Directions:

1. Place the mixed frozen berries, sliced banana, Greek yogurt, freshly squeezed orange juice, rolled oats, and honey into the blender.
2. Blend on high speed until smooth. If you're using spinach, add it to the blender now.
3. If the smoothie is too thick, add a little more orange juice or water to achieve the desired consistency, and blend again.
4. If you would prefer a sweeter drink, taste and add extra honey.
5. After transferring the smoothie into glasses, serve it right away.

Oats & Cinnamon Start

This Oats & Cinnamon Start smoothie is a hearty and wholesome breakfast blend that caters to those looking for a nutritious and satisfying morning treat. With the comfort of cinnamon and the sustaining power of oats, this smoothie is ideal for kicking off a busy day with enduring energy.

Equipment:

Blender, Measuring Cups, Measuring Spoons

Ingredients:

- 1 cup almond milk, unsweetened
- 1/2 cup rolled oats
- 1 banana, ripe and sliced
- 1/4 tsp ground cinnamon
- One tablespoon honey
- 1/2 cup Greek yogurt (use dairy-free if desired)
- 1 tbsp chia seeds
- A pinch of salt
- Ice cubes (optional for a colder smoothie)

Tips:

Soak the oats in the almond milk for 10-15 minutes before blending if you have time; this can make the smoothie even creamier. Sprinkle a little extra cinnamon on top for an added boost of flavor and decoration.

Nutritional Information:

Calories: 295, Protein: 11g, Carbohydrates: 45g, Fat: 8g, Fiber: 7g, Cholesterol: 5 mg, Sodium: 115 mg, Potassium: 422 mg

2 SERVINGS   **5 MINUTES**

Directions:

1. After adding the rolled oats to the blender, process until the mixture resembles flour.
2. Add the almond milk, banana slices, cinnamon, honey, Greek yogurt, chia seeds, and a pinch of salt to the blender with the ground oats.
3. Add a couple ice cubes to the smoothie mixture if you'd like it cooler.
4. Blend on high until all the ingredients are fully combined and the smoothie has a smooth, creamy texture.
5. Taste and add a bit extra honey or maple syrup to adjust the sweetness if needed.
6. For the freshest flavor, pour the smoothie into two glasses and serve right away.

Peachy Keen Sunrise

Awaken your senses with the vibrant hue and refreshing flavors of Peachy Keen Sunrise. This delectable smoothie blend combines the sweetness of ripe peaches with the tanginess of orange juice and the creamy texture of Greek yogurt. It's perfect for a bright start to your day or a nutritious mid-morning snack.

Equipment:
Blender, Measuring Cups, Measuring Spoons

Ingredients:
- 2 cups fresh or frozen peaches, sliced
- 1/2 cup orange juice, freshly squeezed
- 1/2 cup Greek yogurt, plain or vanilla
- 1/4 cup rolled oats
- 1 tablespoon honey, or to taste
- 1/2 teaspoon vanilla extract
- 1/4 teaspoon ground cinnamon
- 4-6 ice cubes (optional, or use if peaches are fresh)

Tips:
Before blending, you can add a spoonful of chia seeds or a scoop of your preferred protein powder to the mixture to increase its nutritional content. If peaches are not in season, frozen ones work just as well and give the smoothie a chilled touch.

Nutritional Information:
Calories: 202, Protein: 8g, Carbohydrates: 38g, Fat: 2g, Fiber: 4g, Cholesterol: 6 mg, Sodium: 21 mg, Potassium: 519 mg

2 SERVINGS   **10 MINUTES**

Directions:
1. Place the peaches, orange juice, Greek yogurt, rolled oats, honey, vanilla extract, ground cinnamon, and ice cubes (if using) into the blender.
2. Blend on a high-speed setting until the mixture is smooth and creamy, making sure the oats are fully incorporated.
3. If the smoothie is too thick, add a little more orange juice or water to reach your desired consistency. If it's not sweet enough, add a bit more honey to taste.
4. Transfer the blended smoothie mixture between two glasses and, if like, top with a sprinkling of cinnamon or a thin peach slice. Serve immediately.

Banana Nut Morning

Wake up to the comforting flavors of a Banana Nut Morning smoothie that feels like a sweet indulgence yet is packed with nutrients to kickstart your day. This luscious blend combines the creaminess of bananas with the heartiness of nuts, creating a rich and satisfying breakfast treat.

Equipment:
Blender, Measuring Cups, Measuring Spoons

Ingredients:
- 2 ripe Bananas, peeled and sliced
- 2 tablespoons Almond Butter
- 1 cup Almond Milk, unsweetened
- 1/4 cup Rolled Oats
- 2 teaspoons Honey (or to taste)
- 1/2 teaspoon Vanilla Extract
- 1/4 teaspoon Ground Cinnamon
- 4 Ice Cubes
- 1 tablespoon Chopped Walnuts, for garnish (optional)

Tips:
For an extra protein boost, add a scoop of your favorite vanilla or unflavored protein powder. If you like your smoothies colder, use frozen banana slices instead of fresh ones.

Nutritional Information:
Calories: 280, Protein: 6g, Carbohydrates: 40g, Fat: 12g, Fiber: 5g, Cholesterol: 0 mg, Sodium: 80 mg, Potassium: 422 mg

2 SERVINGS   5 MINUTES

Directions:
1. Place bananas, almond butter, almond milk, rolled oats, honey, vanilla extract, and cinnamon into the blender.
2. Blend on high speed until all ingredients are well incorporated and the mixture is smooth.
3. Once the smoothie reaches the right consistency, add the ice cubes to the blender and process.
4. Transfer the smoothie between two glasses and, if like, top with chopped walnuts.
5. Serve immediately and enjoy the burst of energy and flavor to start your day!

Apple Pie Energizer

Start your day with the comforting flavors of apple pie in this energizing smoothie. This blend combines the sweet and tartness of green apples with the warmth of cinnamon and the richness of Greek yogurt for a creamy and satisfying breakfast on the go.

Equipment:

Blender, Measuring Cups, Measuring Spoons

Ingredients:

- 1 large Green apple, cored and chopped
- 1/2 cup Plain Greek yogurt
- 1 cup Almond milk, unsweetened
- 1/4 cup Rolled oats
- 2 tbsp Almonds, raw
- 1 tsp Cinnamon, ground
- 1 tbsp Maple syrup or honey (optional for sweetness)
- 1/2 tsp Vanilla extract
- 4-5 Ice cubes (or as needed)
- A pinch of Nutmeg

Tips:

For an even more authentic apple pie flavor, add a small cooked and cooled slice of apple pie into the blender, or a dash of apple pie spice. To boost protein content, feel free to add a scoop of your favorite vanilla protein powder.

Nutritional Information:

Calories: 235, Protein: 10g, Carbohydrates: 33g, Fat: 7g, Fiber: 5g, Cholesterol: 5 mg, Sodium: 95 mg, Potassium: 345 mg

2 SERVINGS **10 MINUTES**

Directions:

1. Place the green apple, Greek yogurt, almond milk, rolled oats, almonds, cinnamon, maple syrup (if using), vanilla extract, ice cubes, and a pinch of nutmeg in a blender.
2. Blend on high until smooth and creamy. To get the right consistency, you can add a little extra almond milk if the smoothie is too thick.
3. If needed, adjust the sweetness or spices based on your taste.
4. Before serving, divide the smoothie between two glasses and top with a little sprinkling of cinnamon.

Tangy Orange Daybreak

Begin your day with a citrus burst that awakens the senses and infuses your morning with energy. "Tangy Orange Daybreak" is a zesty and refreshing smoothie that combines fresh oranges with creamy yogurt and a kiss of ginger for a naturally sweet and invigorating breakfast treat.

Equipment:

Blender, Citrus Juicer (optional), Glasses

Ingredients:

- 1 1/2 cups fresh orange juice (about 3-4 medium oranges, juiced)
- 1 medium banana, sliced and frozen
- 1/2 cup plain Greek yogurt
- 1 tbsp honey, or to taste
- 1/2 tsp fresh ginger, grated
- 1/4 tsp turmeric powder
- Ice cubes (as needed for desired consistency)
- Optional garnish: orange slices, mint leaves

Tips:

Consider adding a scoop of your preferred vanilla or unflavored protein powder for an additional protein boost. To add fiber, a tablespoon of ground flaxseed or chia seeds would be a perfect mix-in.

Nutritional Information:

Calories: 190, Protein: 8g, Carbohydrates: 42g, Fat: 1g, Fiber: 3g, Cholesterol: 5 mg, Sodium: 25 mg, Potassium: 663 mg

2 SERVINGS   10 MINUTES

Directions:

1. Prepare fresh orange juice using a citrus juicer or by squeezing the oranges manually. Ensure all seeds are removed.
2. Place the frozen banana slices, Greek yogurt, honey, grated ginger, and turmeric powder in the blender.
3. Add the fresh orange juice to the blender over the other ingredients.
4. Process the mixture at high speed until it becomes creamy and smooth. Increase the amount of orange juice or add a little water if the smoothie is too thick. Blend again after adding a few ice cubes if it's too thin..
5. If more honey is needed, taste and adjust the sweetness.
6. If more honey is needed, taste and adjust the sweetness.

Cherry Almond Boost

Kickstart your morning with this vibrant, nutrient-packed smoothie that conjures the flavor of a cherry almond pastry in a healthy, sippable form. The sweetness of the cherries is perfectly balanced with the nutty undertones from the almonds and the vanilla, making it an irresistible breakfast treat that's both refreshing and satisfying.

Equipment:

Blender, Measuring Cups, Measuring Spoons

Ingredients:

- 1 cup frozen cherries
- 1 large banana, sliced and frozen
- 2 tablespoons almond butter
- 1 cup unsweetened almond milk
- 1/2 teaspoon pure vanilla extract
- 1 tablespoon honey or to taste (optional)
- 1/4 cup Greek yogurt (for added protein, optional)
- 2 tablespoons ground almonds (for garnish, optional)
- A handful of ice cubes (if a thicker consistency is desired)

Tips:

If cherries aren't in season or you can't find frozen ones, you can substitute with other berries or fruits of your choice. Add a scoop of your favorite protein powder or a handful of spinach to the mixture for an extra nutritional boost; the cherry flavor will help to disguise the greens.

Nutritional Information:

Calories: 215, Protein: 4g, Carbohydrates: 30g, Fat: 10g, Fiber: 5g, Cholesterol: 0 mg, Sodium: 95 mg, Potassium: 382 mg

2 SERVINGS **5 MINUTES**

Directions:

1. Place the frozen cherries, banana slices, almond butter, almond milk, vanilla extract, and honey (if using) into the blender.
2. Blend on high until the ingredients are smooth and creamy.
3. If necessary, add a bit more honey after tasting to regulate the sweetness.
4. To achieve the correct consistency, combine the smoothie again after adding a handful of ice cubes.
5. Pour the smoothie into serving glasses.
6. If desired, garnish with a sprinkle of ground almonds on top.
7. Serve immediately and enjoy your refreshing Cherry Almond Boost.

Avocado Toast Smoothie

This Avocado Toast Smoothie encapsulates the essence of the beloved breakfast staple in a refreshing and creamy drink. With the satisfying flavors of avocado and a subtle hint of toast, it is perfect for those mornings when you're short on time but still crave that classic avocado toast experience.

Equipment:
Blender, Measuring Cups, Measuring Spoons

Ingredients:
- 1 ripened medium avocado, pitted and scooped
- 1 1/2 cups almond milk or preferred plant-based milk
- 1 small frozen banana
- 1/4 cup rolled oats
- 1 tbsp chia seeds
- 1 tbsp almond butter
- 1 tsp pure vanilla extract
- 2 tsp maple syrup, or to taste
- Pinch of salt
- 1/2 cup ice cubes
- Optional: Toasted whole-grain bread crumbs or wheat germ for garnish

Tips:
Add a scoop of your preferred vanilla protein powder for an additional protein boost. Adjust the sweetness by adding more or less maple syrup according to your taste.

Nutritional Information:
Calories: 345, Protein: 6g, Carbohydrates: 37g, Fat: 21g, Fiber: 12g, Cholesterol: 0 mg, Sodium: 180 mg, Potassium: 708 mg

2 SERVINGS   **5 MINUTES**

Directions:
1. Place the avocado, almond milk, frozen banana, rolled oats, chia seeds, almond butter, vanilla extract, maple syrup, salt, and ice cubes into the blender.
2. Process at high speed until creamy and smooth. To get the right consistency, thin out any extra smoothie by adding a small amount of almond milk.
3. Pour the smoothie into glasses. If desired, sprinkle with toasted whole-grain bread crumbs or wheat germ to mimic the texture of toast.
4. Serve immediately and enjoy your Avocado Toast Smoothie as a delightful start to the day.

Seasonal Smoothies

Spring Melon Medley

A refreshing and hydrating smoothie that captures the essence of spring with its fresh melon flavors and vibrant appearance – perfect for a sunny spring morning or a relaxing afternoon treat.

Equipment:
Blender, Measuring Cups and Spoons, Knife, Cutting Board

Ingredients:
- 2 cups Cubed honeydew melon (chilled)
- 1 cup Cubed cantaloupe (chilled)
- 1/2 cup Cucumber (peeled, deseeded and chopped)
- 1/2 cup Fresh spinach leaves
- 6-8 Fresh mint leaves
- 1 tablespoon Lime juice
- 1/2 cup Greek yogurt (plain)
- Half a cup of coconut water or regular water, depending on the consistency you want
- Honey or agave syrup to taste (optional)
- Ice cubes (optional for a colder smoothie)

Tips:
For an extra boost of protein, add a scoop of your favorite vanilla protein powder. To make this smoothie vegan, use plant-based yogurt and agave syrup as the sweetener.

Nutritional Information:
Calories: 150, Protein: 5g, Carbohydrates: 30g, Fat: 1g, Fiber: 3g, Cholesterol: 5 mg, Sodium: 50 mg, Potassium: 680 mg

2 SERVINGS   **10 MINUTES**

Directions:
1. Wash the spinach leaves and mint leaves thoroughly. Peel and chop the cucumber. Cube the honeydew and cantaloupe melons after removing seeds and skin.
2. Place the cubed honeydew melon, cubed cantaloupe, chopped cucumber, spinach leaves, and mint leaves into the blender.
3. Add in the lime juice, Greek yogurt, and coconut water. If sweeter taste is desired, add honey or agave syrup to taste.
4. Blend on high speed until all the ingredients are combined and the mixture is smooth. Add more coconut water to the smoothie if it's too thick to get the right consistency.
5. If preferred chillier, add ice cubes and blend again until smoothie reaches an icy consistency.
6. Taste and adjust sweetness if necessary.
7. Pour into glasses and serve immediately.

Summer Berry Splash

Dive into summer with this vibrant, refreshing smoothie that's bursting with the flavors of the season. The Summer Berry Splash is a delightful blend of juicy berries, creamy yogurt, and a hint of mint, creating a perfectly balanced and nutritious drink that cools you down on a hot day.

Equipment:

Blender, Measuring Cups, Measuring Spoons

Ingredients:

- 1 cup strawberries, hulled
- 1/2 cup raspberries
- 1/2 cup blueberries
- 1/2 banana, sliced
- 3/4 cup plain Greek yogurt
- 1/2 cup orange juice
- 1 tbsp honey (optional, to taste)
- 5-6 fresh mint leaves
- 1/2 cup ice cubes (optional for a colder smoothie)
- Garnish with mint leaves and fresh berries (optional)

Tips:

For a non-dairy version, substitute Greek yogurt with almond or coconut yogurt. If berries are out of season, frozen berries work just as well and help chill the smoothie without the need for ice.

Nutritional Information:

Calories: 162, Protein: 9g, Carbohydrates: 31g, Fat: 1g, Fiber: 5g, Cholesterol: 5 mg, Sodium: 36 mg, Potassium: 460 mg

2 SERVINGS **5 MINUTES**

Directions:

1. Place strawberries, raspberries, blueberries, and banana in the blender.
2. Add in the Greek yogurt and orange juice to help blend smoothly.
3. If a sweeter taste is desired, incorporate the honey into the mixture.
4. Toss in the mint leaves for a fresh, aromatic twist.
5. Include ice cubes if a colder drink is preferred.
6. Blend on high until all ingredients are well combined and the texture is smooth.
7. Transfer the smoothie between two glasses and, if desired, top with extra berries and mint leaves.

Autumn Pumpkin Patch Smoothie

Enjoy the comforting tastes of autumn by sipping on the Autumn Pumpkin Patch Smoothie. Reminiscent of a breezy stroll through a pumpkin patch, this rich and creamy delicacy mixes the traditional flavor of pumpkin with a dash of spice and a splash of maple. A perfect treat that brings the essence of autumn straight to your glass.

Equipment:
Blender, Measuring cups and spoons, Glasses for serving

Ingredients:
- 1 cup Pumpkin puree (canned or fresh)
- 1 1/2 cups almond milk, or any other type of milk
- 1/4 cup Greek yogurt (plain or vanilla)
- 2 Tbsp Maple syrup
- 1/2 tsp Vanilla extract
- 1/2 tsp Pumpkin pie spice
- 1 large Banana (frozen and sliced)
- 1/2 cup Ice cubes (optional, for an extra chill)
- Whipped cream (optional, for garnish)
- A pinch of Cinnamon (optional, for garnish)

Tips:
For added protein and a nuttier flavor, include a tablespoon of almond butter. If you desire more sweetness, adjust the amount of maple syrup, or add a couple of pitted dates before blending.

Nutritional Information:
Calories: 231, Protein: 5g, Carbohydrates: 48g, Fat: 3g, Fiber: 5g, Cholesterol: 3 mg, Sodium: 101 mg, Potassium: 429 mg

2 SERVINGS **10 MINUTES**

Directions:
1. Place the pumpkin puree, almond milk, Greek yogurt, maple syrup, vanilla extract, pumpkin pie spice, and banana in the blender.
2. Blend on high until the mixture is smooth and creamy. Depending on the strength of your blender, this could take 1-2 minutes.
3. Add the ice cubes, if using, and combine once more to get the right consistency. Increase the amount of ice or frozen banana in your smoothie if you'd like it thicker.
4. Transfer the smoothie into cups for serving. Add some cinnamon and a dollop of whipped cream as decoration, if you'd like.
5. Serve immediately and savor the taste of autumn in every sip.

Winter Citrus Zest Fondue

Dive into a warm winter treat with the Winter Citrus Zest Fondue smoothie. This concoction embraces the bold flavors of winter fruits, combined with the creamy backdrop of white chocolate, creating a velvety dip that's perfect for any festive gathering or cozy night in.

Equipment:

Double Boiler, Fondue Pot, Whisk

Ingredients:

- 8 oz White Chocolate, chopped
- 1/4 cup Heavy Cream
- Zest of 1 Orange
- Zest of 1 Lemon
- 2 tbsp Orange Liqueur or Orange Juice
- Assorted Winter Fruits (apple slices, pear slices, banana chunks, whole strawberries) for dipping
- Optional: Crushed Nuts or Desiccated Coconut for garnish

Tips:

For a non-alcoholic version, omit the orange liqueur and use orange juice. Keep the fondue warm to maintain a smooth consistency for dipping.

Nutritional Information:

Calories: 430, Protein: 3g, Carbohydrates: 44g, Fat: 27g, Fiber: 0g, Cholesterol: 41 mg, Sodium: 36 mg, Potassium: 164 mg

4 SERVINGS **15 MINUTES**

Directions:

1. Set up your double boiler by filling the bottom pot with an inch or two of water, and place it over medium heat. Once the water begins to simmer, place the chopped white chocolate and heavy cream in the top pot, ensuring that the water in the bottom does not touch the bottom of the top pot.
2. Stir the chocolate and cream mixture occasionally with a whisk as the white chocolate begins to melt. Make sure the mixture is smooth and well incorporated.
3. Once melted, remove the chocolate mixture from the heat and stir in the zest of the orange and lemon to infuse the citrus flavors into the fondue.
4. Add the orange liqueur or orange juice to the mixture and stir until everything is well combined.
5. Carefully pour the mixture into a pre-warmed fondue pot and set it over a low flame to keep warm.
6. Arrange the assorted winter fruits on a serving platter around the fondue pot. Provide fondue skewers or forks for dipping.
7. If desired, sprinkle crushed nuts or desiccated coconut over the fruit for an added texture.

Harvest Apple Cinnamon Swirl

Fresh from the orchard, this Harvest Apple Cinnamon Swirl smoothie enraptures the palate with the quintessential flavors of fall. Cinnamon spices paired with creamy yogurt and crisp apples blend into a velvety concoction that's both comforting and refreshing. It's like sipping on a cool autumn breeze with a hint of warm holiday joy.

Equipment:
Blender, Measuring Cups, Knife

Ingredients:
- 2 Medium-sized, ripe apples, cored and sliced
- 1 Cup plain or vanilla yogurt
- 1/2 Cup milk or plant-based milk alternative
- 1 Tablespoon honey or maple syrup
- Half a teaspoon of ground cinnamon and a small sprinkle for decoration
- 1/4 Teaspoon vanilla extract
- 1 Cup ice cubes
- Whipped cream (optional, for garnish)
- Cinnamon stick (optional, for garnish)

Tips:
Choose a variety of apple that is sweet and crisp, such as Honeycrisp or Gala, for the best flavor. For a dairy-free version, use a plant-based yogurt and milk alternative. If you desire a colder smoothie, freeze your apple slices beforehand.

Nutritional Information:
Calories: 180, Protein: 5g, Carbohydrates: 36g, Fat: 2g, Fiber: 4g, Cholesterol: 10 mg, Sodium: 70 mg, Potassium: 300 mg

2 SERVINGS | **10 MINUTES**

Directions:
1. Place the sliced apples, yogurt, milk, honey or maple syrup, ground cinnamon, and vanilla extract into the blender.
2. Blend on high until the mixture is smooth and the apples are fully incorporated.
3. Once the ice cubes are in the blender, pulse them until the smoothie has the consistency you want. You can tweak by adding extra milk if you would want your smoothie to be thinner.
4. Divide the smoothie between two glasses. For a pretty presentation, you can add a cinnamon stick, a dollop of whipped cream, and a sprinkling of cinnamon to the top of each glass.

Tropical Mango Rapture

Experience the bliss of the tropics with this creamy and vibrant Tropical Mango Rapture smoothie. Perfect for reminding you of warmer, sun-kissed climates, no matter what the season outside.

Equipment:
Blender, Measuring Cups, Knife

Ingredients:
- 1 cup Fresh Mango Chunks
- 1/2 cup Pineapple Chunks
- 1/2 cup Coconut Milk
- 1 Banana, sliced
- 1/2 cup Orange Juice
- 2 tsp Honey (optional, for added sweetness)
- 6-8 Ice Cubes
- A little amount of recently grated nutmeg (as a garnish)

Tips:
For an extra smooth texture, ensure your mango and pineapple are ripe. If you want a thinner consistency, add a bit more orange juice. This smoothie can also be a fantastic base for a nutritious breakfast bowl; just reduce the liquid to thicken it up and add your favorite toppings.

Nutritional Information:
Calories: 215, Protein: 2g, Carbohydrates: 35g, Fat: 8g, Fiber: 3g, Cholesterol: 0 mg, Sodium: 17 mg, Potassium: 487 mg

2 SERVINGS **10 MINUTES**

Directions:
1. Peel and slice the mango and banana. Measure out your pineapple chunks, coconut milk, and orange juice.
2. Place the mango chunks, pineapple chunks, banana slices, and ice cubes into the blender.
3. Over the fruit in the blender, drizzle the orange juice and coconut milk.
4. If you want a sweeter taste, add more honey.
5. Blend on high until the mixture is smooth and creamy.
6. Taste the smoothie and adjust the honey if needed, blending again if more is added.
7. Transfer the smoothie between two glasses and add a dash of nutmeg to bring out the tropical notes.

Cozy Pear Ginger Blend

Warm up your senses with this delightfully comforting Pear Ginger Blend. The combination of ripe pears, fiery ginger, and a touch of cinnamon offers a harmonious balance of sweetness and spice, perfect for chilly evenings or crisp autumn days. This smoothie feels like a heartwarming hug for your soul.

Equipment:
Blender, Measuring Cups, Measuring Spoons

Ingredients:
- 2 medium Ripe Pears, cored and sliced
- 1 tablespoon Fresh Ginger, grated
- 1 cup Almond Milk, unsweetened
- 1/2 teaspoon Ground Cinnamon
- 1 tablespoon Honey, or to taste
- 1 teaspoon Vanilla Extract
- 1/2 cup Greek Yogurt, plain
- 1/4 cup Rolled Oats
- 4-5 Ice Cubes (optional, or use frozen pears for a colder smoothie)
- A pinch of Salt

Tips:
For added texture, garnish with a sprinkle of cinnamon or a few slices of pear. If you prefer a vegan option, substitute the Greek yogurt with a non-dairy yogurt and use maple syrup instead of honey.

Nutritional Information:
Calories: 210, Protein: 7g, Carbohydrates: 44g, Fat: 2g, Fiber: 6g, Cholesterol: 5 mg, Sodium: 80 mg, Potassium: 345 mg

2 SERVINGS **10 MINUTES**

Directions:
1. Place the sliced pears, grated ginger, almond milk, ground cinnamon, honey, vanilla extract, Greek yogurt, rolled oats, ice cubes (if using), and a pinch of salt into the blender.
2. Process the ingredients at a high speed until it becomes creamy and smooth. To get the right consistency, thin out any extra smoothie by adding a small amount of almond milk.
3. If necessary, add more honey after tasting to regulate the sweetness.
4. Transfer the combined drink into a pair of glasses and promptly serve.

Berry Cherry Jubilee Smoothie

A sumptuous blend of berries and cherries, this smoothie captures the essence of summer with its vibrant hues and tantalizing, sweet flavors. Perfectly chilled and brimming with antioxidants, it's a delightful treat to beat the heat.

Equipment:

Blender, Measuring cups, Glasses

Ingredients:

- 1 cup frozen cherries
- 1/2 cup mixed berries (strawberries, raspberries, blueberries)
- 1/2 banana, sliced
- 1 cup almond milk, unsweetened
- 1/2 cup Greek yogurt, plain
- 1 tablespoon honey, or to taste
- A pinch of ground cinnamon
- Fresh mint leaves for garnish (optional)

Tips:

For an extra protein boost, consider adding a scoop of your favorite protein powder. You can also adjust the sweetness by adding more or less honey to suit your preference, or even substitute with maple syrup or agave nectar.

Nutritional Information:

Calories: 189, Protein: 8g, Carbohydrates: 34g, Fat: 3g, Fiber: 4g, Cholesterol: 8 mg, Sodium: 95 mg, Potassium: 440 mg

2 SERVINGS   5 MINUTES

Directions:

1. Place the frozen cherries, mixed berries, banana, almond milk, Greek yogurt, and honey in the blender.
2. Blend on high until the mixture is smooth and creamy. Add a bit more almond milk if you prefer a thinner consistency.
3. Add a pinch of ground cinnamon and blend for a few more seconds to incorporate.
4. Pour into glasses and garnish with fresh mint leaves if desired.
5. Serve right away, and savor every sip of the cool summer flavor!

Kid-Friendly Creations

Strawberry Banana Smile

This Strawberry Banana Smile smoothie is a cheerful and nutritious blend designed to delight kids of all ages. Brimming with fruity flavors and creamy textures, it's a guaranteed hit for breakfast, snack time, or as a refreshing dessert. This traditional berry-banana dish is a great way to teach kids about the benefits of having a balanced diet!

Equipment:
Blender, Measuring Cups, Measuring Spoons

Ingredients:
- 2 cups fresh strawberries, hulled
- 2 ripe bananas
- 1 cup milk (or plant-based alternative for dairy-free option)
- Half a cup of Greek yogurt, or yogurt without dairy
- 1 tablespoon honey, or to taste (optional)
- 1 cup ice cubes

Tips:
For an extra fun twist, garnish the smoothie with a small skewer of sliced strawberries and bananas on top of each glass. To make the smoothie colder and more slush-like, use frozen strawberries or bananas instead of fresh.

Nutritional Information:
Calories: 145, Protein: 4g, Carbohydrates: 30g, Fat: 2g, Fiber: 3g, Cholesterol: 8 mg, Sodium: 42 mg, Potassium: 472 mg

4 SERVINGS   10 MINUTES

Directions:
1. Place the hulled strawberries, peeled bananas, milk, Greek yogurt, and honey (if using) into the blender.
2. Add in the ice cubes on top to help push down the ingredients for a smooth blend.
3. Blend at a high speed until the smoothie is creamy and all the components are well blended.
4. Taste and add an extra drizzle of honey if a sweeter smoothie is desired. Blend again briefly if more sweetener is added.
5. Pour the smoothie mixture into glasses and serve immediately with a colorful straw or spoon.

Peanut Butter Jelly Time

The Peanut Butter Jelly Time smoothie is a whimsical take on a classic that brings back the comforting tastes of a peanut butter and jelly sandwich in a creamy, drinkable form. This delectable and entertaining dish makes a wholesome, satisfying, and enjoyable snack that's ideal for youngsters and young at heart.

Equipment:

Blender, Measuring Cups, Spoons, Glasses

Ingredients:

- 2 cups Milk (dairy or non-dairy alternative)
- 1/3 cup Creamy Peanut Butter
- 2 tablespoons Grape Jelly (or preferred flavor)
- 1 medium-sized Frozen Banana, sliced
- 1/2 cup Frozen Strawberries
- 1 tablespoon Honey (optional, for added sweetness)
- 1/2 teaspoon Vanilla Extract
- Whipped Cream for topping (optional)
- Crushed Peanuts for garnish (optional)
- Fresh Strawberries or Grapes for garnish (optional)

Tips:

If you're making this for very young kids, ensure the smoothie is not too thick to avoid any difficulties in drinking. You can also substitute jelly with fresh or frozen berries for a more natural sweetness.

Nutritional Information:

Calories: 300, Protein: 10g, Carbohydrates: 32g, Fat: 16g, Fiber: 3g, Cholesterol: 5 mg, Sodium: 200 mg, Potassium: 400 mg

4 SERVINGS   **5 MINUTES**

Directions:

1. Place milk, creamy peanut butter, grape jelly, frozen banana, frozen strawberries, honey (if using), and vanilla extract into the blender.
2. Process the ingredients at a high speed until the product is smooth and well blended. Add extra milk to the smoothie one tablespoon at a time until the right consistency is achieved if it's too thick.
3. Pour the smoothie evenly into four glasses.
4. Garnish each smoothie with a few pieces of fresh fruit, such as grapes or strawberries, and a dollop of whipped cream, if preferred.
5. Serve immediately and enjoy the taste of a childhood favorite in a new, fun form!

Hidden Veggie Chocolate Surprise

Dive into a decadent chocolate smoothie that packs a nutritious punch! Perfect for sneaking in the goodness of vegetables without the kids even noticing, this creamy creation is a delight for both the young and the young at heart. Indulge in the velvety smoothness of chocolate bliss while feeding your family the nourishment they need.

Equipment:

Blender, Measuring Cups, Measuring Spoons

Ingredients:

- 2 cups unsweetened almond milk
- 1/2 medium ripe avocado
- 1/2 cup baby spinach, packed
- 1 medium ripe banana, frozen
- 2 Tbsp unsweetened cocoa powder
- 3 Tbsp honey, or to taste
- 1/4 cup cooked and pureed sweet potato
- 1/2 tsp vanilla extract
- Ice cubes, as needed for desired consistency
- Whipped cream and grated chocolate (optional for garnish)

Tips:

Make sure all the veggie ingredients are well-blended so there are no noticeable chunks. For a frozen treat, use frozen sweet potato puree and additional ice to make a thicker, frosty version.

Nutritional Information:

Calories: 160, Protein: 2g, Carbohydrates: 24g, Fat: 7g, Fiber: 5g, Cholesterol: 0 mg, Sodium: 90 mg, Potassium: 412 mg

4 SERVINGS **10 MINUTES**

Directions:

1. Place the almond milk, ripe avocado, baby spinach, frozen banana, cocoa powder, honey, sweet potato puree, and vanilla extract into the blender.
2. Blend on high until all the ingredients are thoroughly combined and the mixture is smooth. If the mixture is too thick, add extra almond milk. If it is too thin, add a handful of ice cubes and blend again.
3. For a playful and intriguing presentation, pour the smoothie into glasses and top with a dollop of whipped cream and a sprinkling of grated chocolate, if using.
4. Serve immediately and watch as everyone enjoys their chocolatey treat, completely unaware of the hidden veggies inside!

Apple Orchard Adventure

Dive into the heart of the orchard with this kid-friendly "Apple Orchard Adventure" Fondue! Perfect for little hands and big imaginations, this non-traditional fondue features a luscious, cinnamon-spiced apple and yogurt dip. Watch as children delight in dunking their favorite fruits, marshmallows, or graham crackers into the warm, inviting flavors of a freshly picked apple adventure.

Equipment:

Medium Saucepan, Whisk, Fondue pot (optional), Fondue forks or skewers

Ingredients:

- 2 cups Unsweetened applesauce
- 1 cup Greek yogurt, plain
- 2 tbsp Honey or to taste
- 1/2 tsp Ground cinnamon
- A pinch of Nutmeg
- Fruits such as strawberries, apple slices, and banana slices for dipping
- Marshmallows, graham crackers, or angel food cake pieces for dipping
- Optional toppings: Granola or crushed nuts for texture

Tips:

If you're serving this to very young children, let the mixture cool slightly to ensure it's not too hot for little mouths. For an extra fun twist, let the kids help with cutting the fruits using child-safe knives under adult supervision.

Nutritional Information:

Calories: 155, Protein: 4g, Carbohydrates: 35g, Fat: 1g, Fiber: 3g, Cholesterol: 3 mg, Sodium: 22 mg, Potassium: 202 mg

4 SERVINGS **0 MINUTES**

Directions:

1. In a medium saucepan, combine the unsweetened applesauce, Greek yogurt, honey, ground cinnamon, and a pinch of nutmeg. Stir the ingredients together until you have a smooth mixture.
2. Warm the mixture to the touch but avoid boiling it by placing the pot over medium heat and whisking the mixture occasionally. If desired, increase the amount of honey to adjust the sweetness.
3. Once heated through, transfer the apple-yogurt mixture to a fondue pot to keep warm. If you don't have a fondue pot, simply serve it warm and return to the stove to reheat if necessary.
4. Arrange your chosen fruits, marshmallows, graham crackers, and any additional dipping items on a serving platter.
5. Use fondue forks or skewers to dip the items into the warm apple yogurt mixture. Optionally, sprinkle granola or crushed nuts on top for an added crunch.
6. Encourage kids to mix and match their dipping items to create their own "Apple Orchard Adventure" combinations, and watch the fun unfold!

Tropical Treasure Hunt

Unlock a bounty of flavors with this "Tropical Treasure Hunt" smoothie, perfect for the little explorers in your family. This creamy and vibrant concoction is a delightful blend of tropical fruits and smooth yogurt, sure to set sail for a nutritious adventure in every sip.

Equipment:
Blender, Measuring Cups, Measuring Spoons

Ingredients:
- 1 cup pineapple chunks, frozen
- 1 medium ripe banana
- 1 cup mango chunks, frozen
- 1/2 cup coconut milk
- 1/2 cup orange juice, freshly squeezed
- 1/2 cup Greek yogurt, plain
- 1 tablespoon honey (optional, adjust to taste)
- 2 tablespoons shredded coconut (for garnish)
- Additional tropical fruits (like kiwi or papaya), for garnish (optional)

Tips:
To make this a more interactive experience for kids, you can set up a "treasure garnish bar" with bowls of different tropical fruits and let them top their own smoothies. Freeze any extra smoothie in popsicle molds for a fun frozen treat on another day.

Nutritional Information:
Calories: 180, Protein: 5g, Carbohydrates: 34g, Fat: 3.5g, Fiber: 3g, Cholesterol: 3 mg, Sodium: 20 mg, Potassium: 430 mg

4 SERVINGS **10 MINUTES**

Directions:
1. Place the pineapple, banana, mango, coconut milk, orange juice, and Greek yogurt into the blender.
2. Puree the mixture until smooth. If the mixture is too thick, thin it up with a little extra orange juice or coconut milk.
3. Taste and sweeten with honey if desired. Blend again to mix the sweetener thoroughly.
4. Pour the smoothie into glasses and garnish with shredded coconut and optional fruit garnishes to turn each glass into a treasure-filled island.
5. Serve immediately and watch the little ones embark on a flavor-filled expedition!

Purple Berry Galaxy

Dive into a cosmic blend of flavors with the "Purple Berry Galaxy" smoothie, perfectly crafted for kids and adults alike. This celestial treat combines the sweet and tangy tastes of mixed berries with a creamy base, ensuring a smoothie experience that's out of this world. Its vibrant purple hue is not only appealing to the eye but packed with antioxidants too.

Equipment:

Blender, Measuring Cups, Serving Glasses

Ingredients:

- 1 cup plain or vanilla Greek yogurt
- 2 cups mixed frozen berries (blueberries, strawberries, raspberries, blackberries)
- 1 ripe banana
- half a cup white grape juice or apple juice
- 1 tablespoon honey (optional, depending on sweetness preference)
- 1 teaspoon chia seeds (optional, for an extra nutritional boost)

Tips:

For an even more kid-friendly presentation, garnish with a few fresh berries on top or a fun straw. To make it a dairy-free option, substitute Greek yogurt with a plant-based yogurt or use a dairy-free milk alternative.

Nutritional Information:

Calories: 145, Protein: 7g, Carbohydrates: 28g, Fat: 1g, Fiber: 4g, Cholesterol: 3 mg, Sodium: 20 mg, Potassium: 220 mg

4 SERVINGS   **5 MINUTES**

Directions:

1. Place the Greek yogurt, frozen berries, ripe banana, and juice into the blender.
2. Process the ingredients at a high speed until it becomes creamy and smooth. If it's too thick, you can add a little more juice to reach the desired consistency.
3. Taste the smoothie and add honey if a sweeter taste is desired. Blend again for a few seconds to mix well.
4. Transfer the smoothie into serving glasses and garnish with chia seeds for an added nutritional boost.
5. Enjoy your interstellar voyage in a glass and serve right away for the freshest flavor!

Green Monster Mystery

Dive into a delightful fusion of fruits and greens that will make your taste buds dance and keep the kids coming back for more! The "Green Monster Mystery" smoothie is a clever way to sneak in those nutritious veggies without a fuss. With a naturally sweet taste and a vibrant green color, this smoothie is a hit for both its mysterious allure and its health benefits.

Equipment:
Blender, Measuring cups, Measuring spoons

Ingredients:
- 1 cup fresh spinach leaves
- 1 medium ripe banana, sliced
- 1 cup frozen pineapple chunks
- 1/2 ripe avocado, peeled and pitted
- 1/2 cup Greek yogurt, plain
- 2 tablespoons honey or to taste
- 1 1/2 cups apple juice, chilled
- 1/2 cup ice cubes (optional for a thicker texture)

Tips:
Encourage the kids to help with the preparation by picking the spinach leaves or adding them to the blender; it's a fun way to get them excited about healthy eating. Consider incorporating a handful of chia seeds or a scoop of your preferred protein powder into the mixture to boost its nutritious content.

Nutritional Information:
Calories: 185, Protein: 4g, Carbohydrates: 37g, Fat: 4g, Fiber: 3g, Cholesterol: 2 mg, Sodium: 23 mg, Potassium: 429 mg

4 SERVINGS **10 MINUTES**

Directions:
1. After giving the spinach leaves a thorough rinse to get rid of any dirt, pat them dry.
2. Place the banana, pineapple, avocado, and Greek yogurt into the blender.
3. Add in the honey and apple juice, followed by the spinach leaves on top to help weigh down the ingredients.
4. If a thicker consistency is desired, add the optional ice cubes.
5. Blend on high until all the ingredients are smooth and no chunks remain. If the mixture is too thick, add a little more apple juice to reach the desired consistency.
6. If more honey is needed, taste the smoothie and adjust the sweetness.
7. Pour the Green Monster Mystery smoothie into glasses and serve immediately with fun straws or topped with a slice of fruit for an extra special touch.

Orange Creamsicle Delight

Recall the nostalgic taste of a childhood classic with this Orange Creamsicle Delight! This smooth fondue is a creamy, dreamy combination of zesty orange and smooth vanilla, sure to become a new favorite among the little ones and grown-ups alike. Perfect for dipping fresh fruit or marshmallows, it adds a playful twist to any gathering.

Equipment:

Medium Saucepan, Whisk, Fondue pot (optional)

Ingredients:

- One cup of freshly squeezed orange juice for optimal flavor
- 2 cups white chocolate chips, a sweet and smooth base
- 1/2 cup heavy cream, to add richness
- 1 tbsp unsalted butter, for a silky texture
- 1 tsp vanilla extract, for that classic creamsicle aroma
- To counteract the sweetness, add 1/4 tsp salt
- For serving: assorted fruits like strawberries, bananas, and pineapple; marshmallows; graham crackers

Tips:

If the fondue is too thick, you can thin it with a tablespoon of orange juice at a time until desired consistency is reached. For a fun twist, add a teaspoon of orange zest for a bolder citrus highlight.

Nutritional Information:

Calories: 490, Protein: 3g, Carbohydrates: 50g, Fat: 32g, Fiber: 0g, Cholesterol: 50 mg, Sodium: 95 mg, Potassium: 179 mg

4 SERVINGS   **0 MINUTES**

Directions:

1. In a medium saucepan over low heat, combine the orange juice, heavy cream, and unsalted butter. Gently stir the mixture until the butter melts.
2. Gradually add the white chocolate chips to the saucepan, whisking continuously until the chocolate is fully melted and the mixture is smooth.
3. Add the salt and vanilla essence, stir, and simmer for one more minute, just to make sure everything is properly combined.
4. If using a fondue pot, carefully transfer the mixture to the pot, set over a low flame to keep the Orange Creamsicle Delight warm and smooth for dipping.
5. Arrange the fruits, marshmallows, and graham crackers on a platter for dipping into the delectable fondue.

Diabetic-Friendly Smoothies

Low-Sugar Berry Bliss

Delight in the refreshing zest of the Low-Sugar Berry Bliss, a detox smoothie that melds the tangy flavors of mixed berries with a subtle sweetness, all while keeping sugar content to a minimum. This smoothie's antioxidant-rich nutrients and hydrating components not only tempt your taste senses but also help you achieve your wellness objectives. It's the perfect morning or afternoon pick-me-up to cleanse your palate and rejuvenate your body.

Equipment:
Blender, Measuring Cups, Measuring Spoons

Ingredients:
- 1 cup Unsweetened Almond Milk
- 1/2 cup Mixed Berries (frozen or fresh: blueberries, raspberries, strawberries)
- 1/4 cup Beetroot, chopped fresh or pre-cooked (for natural sweetness and detox benefits)
- 1/2 medium Avocado (for creaminess and healthy fats)
- 1 tbsp Chia Seeds (for fiber and omega-3 fatty acids)
- 1/4 tsp Ground Cinnamon (optional, for added flavor and blood sugar support)
- 1 tsp Fresh Lemon Juice (optional, to brighten the flavors)
- Ice Cubes (optional, for a thicker and cooler smoothie)
- If you want more sweetness without adding sugar, you can add stevia or monk fruit extract to taste.

Tips:
To save time for future preparations, create individual portion bags with berries, beetroot, and avocado, and freeze them. When you're ready to make your smoothie, just grab a bag, add almond milk, chia seeds, and your optional ingredients, and blend.

Nutritional Information:
Calories: 150, Protein: 3g, Carbohydrates: 12g, Fat: 10g, Fiber: 6g, Cholesterol: 0 mg, Sodium: 80 mg, Potassium: 345 mg

2 SERVINGS   **10 MINUTES**

Directions:
1. Begin by measuring out and preparing your ingredients, ensuring berries are washed and avocados are pitted and scooped.
2. In the blender, combine the unsweetened almond milk, mixed berries, and chopped beetroot.
3. Add the half medium avocado and chia seeds into the mixture.
4. If you're using ground cinnamon and lemon juice, add them now for an extra burst of flavor.
5. Blend on high until all ingredients are well combined and the texture is smooth. For a thicker consistency, add ice cubes and blend again.
6. Taste your smoothie and if you desire a bit more sweetness, add a small amount of Stevia or Monk Fruit extract, then blend briefly once more to mix through.
7. Pour into glasses and enjoy immediately for optimal freshness and potency.

Cinnamon Apple Balance

Embark on a sweet and spicy journey with the Cinnamon Apple Balance smoothie, your perfect ally for a detoxifying and satisfying treat. This nutrient-rich drink, enhanced by the warm, energizing sensation of cinnamon and the inherent sweetness of apples, is a treat for your taste buds as well as a health benefit.

Equipment:

Blender, Measuring Cups, Measuring Spoons

Ingredients:

- 2 Medium Apples, cored and sliced
- 1 Banana, sliced
- 1 Cup Fresh Spinach
- 1 Tablespoon Chia Seeds
- 1/4 Teaspoon Ground Cinnamon
- 1 Tablespoon Honey (optional, for added sweetness)
- 1 Cup Almond Milk, unsweetened
- 1/2 Cup Ice Cubes
- A pinch of Salt (to enhance flavors)

Tips:

For a cooler smoothie, you can freeze the banana slices before blending. Add extra almond milk a little at a time until you get the texture you want if you like your consistency thinner. Try adding a small teaspoon of ginger or nutmeg to add another dimension of taste.

Nutritional Information:

Calories: 195, Protein: 3g, Carbohydrates: 40g, Fat: 4g, Fiber: 7g, Cholesterol: 0 mg, Sodium: 95 mg, Potassium: 422 mg.

2 SERVINGS   **10 MINUTES**

Directions:

1. Place all the sliced apples, banana, and fresh spinach into the blender.
2. Add the chia seeds, ground cinnamon, honey (if using), and a pinch of salt to the mix.
3. To make sure the smoothie is cool and energizing, pour in the unsweetened almond milk and top with ice chips.
4. Using a spatula to scrape down the sides as needed, blend on high speed until smooth and creamy.
5. Taste and adjust the sweetness or cinnamon to your liking. If the smoothie is too thick, add a little more almond milk to reach the desired consistency.
6. Transfer the mixture between two glasses and, if like, top with a little amount of chia seeds or cinnamon.

Creamy Avocado Dream

Indulge in a smooth and fulfilling mixture that not only entices your palate but also helps you achieve your detoxification objectives. The Creamy Avocado Dream smoothie is a symphony of creamy texture and refreshing flavors, packed with nutrients to cleanse and nourish your body.

Equipment:

Blender, Measuring cups, Knife

Ingredients:

- 1 ripe Avocado, peeled and pitted
- 1 cup Almond milk, unsweetened
- 1/2 cup Fresh spinach, packed
- 1 small Banana, frozen
- 1 tbsp Chia seeds
- 1 tbsp Fresh lemon juice
- 1 tsp Fresh ginger, grated
- 1/2 tsp maple syrup or honey
- Ice cubes (optional, for a thicker smoothie)

Tips:

For an extra detox boost, add a handful of kale or a tablespoon of spirulina to the recipe. Always start with a little bit, taste, and then add more to ensure the flavor stays balanced to your liking.

Nutritional Information:

Calories: 235, Protein: 4g, Carbohydrates: 21g, Fat: 16g, Fiber: 9g, Cholesterol: 0 mg, Sodium: 98 mg, Potassium: 690 mg

2 SERVINGS **10 MINUTES**

Directions:

1. Place the avocado, almond milk, spinach, frozen banana, chia seeds, lemon juice, and grated ginger into your blender.
2. Process on high until the mixture is smooth and creamy and all the components are well mixed.
3. After tasting the smoothie, you may add honey or maple syrup to taste it a little sweeter. Blend again for a few seconds to mix in the sweetener.
4. Add a few ice cubes if you want your smoothie to be thicker, and blend until the consistency you want is achieved.
5. Pour the Creamy Avocado Dream smoothie into glasses and enjoy immediately for the freshest flavor and most potent nutrients.

Ginger Peach Soothe

Discover the soothing blend of fresh ginger and ripe peaches in this detox smoothie. Its invigorating flavor will awaken your senses and provide a gentle cleanse that's perfect for any time of the day.

Equipment:

Blender, Measuring Cups, Measuring Spoons

Ingredients:

- 2 Cups Frozen Peach Slices
- 1 Tbsp Fresh Ginger, grated
- 1 Cup Spinach Leaves, packed
- 1 Tbsp Chia Seeds
- 2 Tbsp Honey, or to taste (optional)
- 1 Cup Almond Milk, unsweetened
- 1/2 Lemon, juiced
- 1/2 Cup Cold Water, or as needed for desired consistency

Tips:

To chill the smoothie, if using fresh peaches, you might want to add a few ice cubes to the blender. Any plant-based milk can be used in place of almond milk if you have different nutritional requirements or want a different flavor.

Nutritional Information:

Calories: 190, Protein: 3g, Carbohydrates: 39g, Fat: 3g, Fiber: 5g, Cholesterol: 0 mg, Sodium: 85 mg, Potassium: 422 mg

2 SERVINGS **10 MINUTES**

Directions:

1. Place the frozen peach slices, grated fresh ginger, spinach leaves, and chia seeds into the blender.
2. Add honey (if using) for sweetness, the fresh lemon juice, and unsweetened almond milk to the mixture.
3. Begin blending on low, gradually increasing the speed to high until all components are well combined and smooth.
4. If the smoothie is too thick, add cold water in small increments and continue to blend until you reach your preferred consistency.
5. Once again, blend for a short while after tasting and, if needed, adjusting the sweetness with a bit more honey.
6. After dividing the smoothie between two glasses, serve right away.

Tangy Raspberry Refresh

The Tangy Raspberry Refresh is a lively, zesty detox smoothie that combines the bold tartness of raspberries with the zing of fresh ginger and the citrusy punch of lemon. Packed with antioxidants and vitamin C, this vibrant beverage is perfect for a revitalizing morning start or an invigorating afternoon pick-me-up.

Equipment:

Blender, Measuring cups, Measuring spoons

Ingredients:

- 1 cup fresh raspberries
- 1 medium ripe banana, sliced
- a one-inch-long, freshly peeled and grated piece of ginger
- Juice of 1 lemon
- 2 teaspoons honey (optional, to taste)
- 1 tablespoon chia seeds
- 1 cup spinach leaves, washed
- 1 ½ cups coconut water or filtered water
- Ice cubes (optional, for a chilled smoothie)

Tips:

You can increase the recipe's protein content by adding a scoop of unsweetened protein powder. Also, if raspberries aren't your thing, feel free to swap them out for strawberries or mixed berries!

Nutritional Information:

Calories: 150, Protein: 3g, Carbohydrates: 29g, Fat: 2g, Fiber: 8g, Cholesterol: 0 mg, Sodium: 94 mg, Potassium: 470 mg

2 SERVINGS **10 MINUTES**

Directions:

1. Place the fresh raspberries, banana slices, grated ginger, and lemon juice into the blender.
2. If you're using honey for a touch of natural sweetness, add it to the blender now.
3. Sprinkle in the chia seeds and add the spinach leaves to the mix.
4. Pour the coconut water (or filtered water) over the ingredients and add ice cubes if you'd like a cooler smoothie.
5. Secure the lid of the blender and blend on high speed until everything is thoroughly combined and the mixture is smooth.
6. If more honey is needed, taste the smoothie and adjust the sweetness.
7. Pour the smoothie into two glasses, dividing equally.
8. Serve immediately for the freshest flavor and the most vibrant nutrients.

Kale and Blueberry Burst

Enjoy a refreshing detox smoothie that combines the rich antioxidants of blueberries with the powerhouse of vitamins in kale. This "Kale and Blueberry Burst" is not only delicious but also a great way to kickstart your body's natural cleansing process.

Equipment:

Blender, Measuring Cups, Knife

Ingredients:

- 1 cup fresh kale, chopped
- 3/4 cup blueberries, frozen
- 1 banana, sliced
- 1 tablespoon chia seeds
- 1 tablespoon honey (optional, for added sweetness)
- Half a cup of water or unsweetened almond milk
- 1/2 teaspoon grated ginger
- Juice of 1/2 a lemon
- A couple of ice cubes (if you want your smoothie cooler)

Tips:

If you like your smoothie a bit thinner, adjust the liquid to your preference by adding a little more almond milk or water. To enhance the detox effect, opt for organic produce and consider adding a scoop of your preferred greens powder or a spritz of apple cider vinegar.

Nutritional Information:

Calories: 145, Protein: 3g, Carbohydrates: 32g, Fat: 2g, Fiber: 5g, Cholesterol: 0 mg, Sodium: 51 mg, Potassium: 423 mg

2 SERVINGS   **5 MINUTES**

Directions:

1. Rinse the kale leaves thoroughly and chop them into smaller pieces.
2. Combine the chopped kale, blueberries, banana slices, chia seeds, and grated ginger in the blender.
3. After adding the lemon juice and unsweetened almond milk or water, mix until smooth.
4. Taste and blend in honey if you prefer a sweeter smoothie
5. If you want a colder drink, add in a few ice cubes and blend again until you reach your desired consistency.
6. Pour into glasses and serve immediately.

Chia Seed Citrus Fusion

Infuse your detox routine with the vibrant Chia Seed Citrus Fusion. A zesty blend of refreshing citrus and powerful chia seeds make this smoothie an essential pick-me-up that cleanses and revitalizes the body from within. Perfect as a morning boost or an after-workout refresher.

Equipment:

Blender, Measuring spoons, Glasses

Ingredients:

- 1 cup Fresh orange juice
- 1/2 Lemon, juiced
- 2 tbsp Chia seeds
- 1/2 cup Water
- One tablespoon honey (optional, for sweetness) or maple syrup
- 1/2 inch Fresh ginger, peeled
- 1 cup Ice cubes
- 1/2 Grapefruit, juiced
- Mint leaves for garnish (optional)

Tips:

Before blending, think about adding a handful of spinach or kale for an extra detox benefit. You can also substitute the water with coconut water for added electrolytes and flavor.

Nutritional Information:

Calories: 160, Protein: 3g, Carbohydrates: 28g, Fat: 5g, Fiber: 6g, Cholesterol: 0 mg, Sodium: 5 mg, Potassium: 300 mg

2 SERVINGS **5 MINUTES**

Directions:

1. In a small bowl, soak the chia seeds in 1/2 cup of water for at least 5 minutes to allow them to swell and form a gel-like consistency.
2. In a blender, combine the fresh orange juice, lemon juice, grapefruit juice, and the ginger.
3. Process the mixture at a high speed until it's smooth.
4. Add the soaked chia seeds and the water they soaked in, and blend for a few more seconds to make sure they are well combined.
5. After tasting the mixture, add honey or maple syrup, if preferred, and blend just long enough to combine.
6. When the smoothie reaches the consistency you like, add the ice cubes and continue blending.
7. Pour the Chia Seed Citrus Fusion into glasses, garnish with mint leaves if using, and enjoy immediately.

Coco-Cucumber Cooler

Clear your system with this refreshing, detoxifying smoothie that combines the hydrating power of cucumber with the tropical essence of coconut water and a zing of ginger. Perfect for a post-workout rehydration or a morning cleanse, the Coco-Cucumber Cooler is a serene sip of balance and rejuvenation.

Equipment:

Blender, Knife, Cutting Board

Ingredients:

- 1 medium Cucumber, sliced
- 2 cups Coconut Water, chilled
- 1 inch Fresh Ginger, grated
- Juice of 1 Lime
- 2 tbsp Fresh Mint Leaves
- 1 tbsp Honey (optional, adjust according to taste)
- 1/2 cup Ice Cubes

Tips:

For a creamier texture, add half an avocado or a scoop of Greek yogurt. To enhance the detoxifying effect, sprinkle in a teaspoon of chia seeds before blending.

Nutritional Information:

Calories: 84, Protein: 2g, Carbohydrates: 18g, Fat: 1g, Fiber: 3g, Cholesterol: 0 mg, Sodium: 252 mg, Potassium: 667 mg

2 SERVINGS **0 MINUTES**

Directions:

1. Wash and slice the cucumber. No need to peel if it's organic or you prefer a richer nutritional content.
2. Grate the ginger finely, avoiding any tough bits of the root.
3. Cucumber slices, freshly grated ginger, coconut water, lime juice, and mint leaves should all be combined in a blender. Add honey if desired for a touch of sweetness.
4. Blend on high speed after adding the ice cubes to the blender until everything is well combined and the texture is smooth.
5. If necessary, taste and adjust the sweetness with honey. If you want additional tang, add a bit extra lime juice.
6. Transfer the mixture into chilled glasses and decorate with a lime wedge or a sprig of mint.

Detox Smoothie

Lemon Ginger Zest

Refreshing and tangy, this Lemon Ginger Zest smoothie is perfect for a revitalizing detox. The zing of ginger complements the tartness of the lemon, creating a vibrant blend that cleanses the palate and awakens the senses.

Equipment:
Blender, Knife, Cutting board

Ingredients:
- 1 cup Water
- 1 Lemon, peeled and seeds removed
- 1/2 inch Ginger root, peeled
- 1 tbsp Honey (optional, or substitute with maple syrup)
- 1/2 cup Cucumber, chopped
- 1 handful Spinach leaves
- 1 scoop Protein powder (optional, plant-based for added nutrients)
- Ice cubes, as desired

Tips:
You can add a tablespoon of apple cider vinegar or a teaspoon of cayenne pepper to your smoothie for an added cleansing effect.

Nutritional Information:
Calories: 58, Protein: 1g, Carbohydrates: 15g, Fat: 0.3g, Fiber: 2.5g, Cholesterol: 0 mg, Sodium: 10 mg, Potassium: 116 mg

2 SERVINGS **10 MINUTES**

Directions:
1. Add water, chopped lemon, ginger, honey (if using), cucumber, spinach, and protein powder (if using) into the blender.
2. Process at a high speed until the liquid is smooth and all the contents are well combined.
3. In the blender, add the ice cubes and pulse until the smoothie becomes the consistency you want.
4. After tasting the smoothie, taste it and add additional honey or maple syrup if necessary to make it more sweet.
5. Pour into two glasses and serve immediately for a fresh, zesty wake-up call for your body.

Apple Cider Vinegar Revive

This Apple Cider Vinegar Revive smoothie is a tangy and refreshing detox beverage that combines the gut-health benefits of apple cider vinegar with the natural sweetness of fruits. Perfect for mornings or a mid-day boost, this smoothie is not only delicious but also aids in digestion and rejuvenation.

Equipment:

Blender, Measuring Cups, Measuring Spoons

Ingredients:

- 1 cup filtered water
- Add "the mother" to two tablespoons of organic apple cider vinegar.
- 1 large green apple, cored and sliced
- 1/2 medium cucumber, chopped
- 1 tbsp fresh lemon juice
- 1 tsp honey or agave syrup (optional for sweetness)
- 1/2 inch ginger root, peeled
- 1 cup ice cubes
- Fresh mint leaves for garnish (optional)

Tips:

Make sure to use organic apple cider vinegar with "the mother" for the maximum health benefits. To increase metabolism and give it a little extra zing, you may also add a pinch of cayenne pepper. Just adjust the sweetness to your taste.

Nutritional Information:

Calories: 95, Protein: 0.5g, Carbohydrates: 23g, Fat: 0.2g, Fiber: 4g, Cholesterol: 0 mg, Sodium: 13 mg, Potassium: 194 mg

2 SERVINGS   **5 MINUTES**

Directions:

1. Place water, apple cider vinegar, green apple slices, cucumber, lemon juice, honey (if using), and ginger root in the blender.
2. Process on high speed for about a minute or until the mixture is smooth.
3. To reach the desired consistency, add the ice cubes to the blender and pulse.
4. If preferred, top the smoothie with fresh mint leaves after pouring it into glasses.
5. Serve immediately and enjoy your detox smoothie.

Cucumber Mint Refresher

For a hydrating and revitalizing detox smoothie that cleanses your palate and invigorates your senses, the "Cucumber Mint Refresher" is a perfect choice. Its refreshing taste comes from the coolness of cucumber and the zesty uplift of fresh mint. It's an ideal drink for a hot day or after a workout to replenish lost fluids and help you feel refreshed.

Equipment:

Blender, Knife, Cutting Board

Ingredients:

- 1 large cucumber, peeled and sliced
- 1 cup fresh spinach leaves, washed
- 1/2 cup fresh mint leaves
- 1 apple, cored and sliced (green apple preferred for tartness)
- Juice of 1 lemon
- 1 tablespoon honey (optional, adjust to taste)
- 1 cup coconut water or plain water, chilled
- Ice cubes (optional, for serving)

Tips:

For an extra cooling effect, freeze the cucumber slices before blending. For a beautiful presentation, you may also add a small slice of cucumber or a sprig of mint to the rim of the glass as a garnish.

Nutritional Information:

Calories: 84, Protein: 2g, Carbohydrates: 20g, Fat: 0.5g, Fiber: 4g, Cholesterol: 0 mg, Sodium: 56 mg, Potassium: 516 mg

2 SERVINGS **10 MINUTES**

Directions:

1. Place cucumber slices, spinach leaves, mint leaves, and apple slices into the blender.
2. Pour lemon juice and chilled coconut water or plain water over the ingredients in the blender.
3. Process at a high speed until the mixture is uniformly smooth. To get the right consistency, add extra water if the mixture is too thick.
4. Taste the smoothie and if desired, add honey for extra sweetness.
5. If you would like a colder beverage, put the ice cubes in the blender and process them until they are completely broken up and blended into the smoothie.
6. Pour the "Cucumber Mint Refresher" into glasses and serve immediately.

Carrot Citrus Purge

The Carrot Citrus Purge is a vibrant detox smoothie that combines the natural sweetness of carrots with the tangy punch of citrus fruits. This smoothie is perfect for those who are looking for a refreshing and nourishing drink to help cleanse their system and boost their vitality.

Equipment:

Blender, Knife, Cutting Board

Ingredients:

- 1 cup Carrots, peeled and chopped
- 1 large Orange, peeled and segmented
- 1/2 Lemon, peeled and seeded
- 1 inch Ginger, peeled and chopped
- 1/4 teaspoon Turmeric, ground
- 1 Tablespoon Flaxseed, ground
- 1 cup Water or Coconut Water
- 1/2 cup Ice Cubes (optional)

Tips:

Add a little more water or coconut water to the smoothie if it's too thick until you have the right consistency. For an additional protein kick, add a scoop of your favorite protein powder.

Nutritional Information:

Calories: 95, Protein: 2g, Carbohydrates: 21g, Fat: 1g, Fiber: 5g, Cholesterol: 0mg, Sodium: 42mg, Potassium: 389mg

2 SERVINGS **10 MINUTES**

Directions:

1. Place the chopped carrots, orange segments, lemon, ginger, and turmeric into the blender.
2. Add the ground flaxseed to the mix for an extra fiber boost.
3. If you want a colder beverage, add ice cubes after adding the water or coconut water.
4. Process on high until the mixture is well-integrated and smooth.
5. Taste and adjust the sweetness or tartness by adding a small amount of natural sweetener (like honey or agave nectar) or more lemon, if necessary.
6. Pour into glasses and serve immediately.

Simple Spinach Detox

Experience the rejuvenating power of a green detox with the Simple Spinach Detox smoothie. Packed with leafy greens and a hint of tropical flavors, this smoothie is not only nourishing but also incredibly refreshing. It's perfect for a quick nutritional boost to help cleanse the body and promote wellness.

Equipment:

Blender, Measuring Cups, Measuring Spoons

Ingredients:

- 2 cups fresh spinach
- 1 ripe banana, sliced and frozen
- 1/2 cup frozen pineapple chunks
- 1 tablespoon chia seeds
- 1 cup unsweetened almond milk (or substitute with coconut water)
- 1/2 inch fresh ginger, peeled and minced
- Juice of 1/2 lemon
- 1 teaspoon honey or agave syrup (optional)

Tips:

For an extra cool and refreshing smoothie, ensure all the fruits are frozen before use. If you want to enhance the detoxifying effects, consider adding a small handful of parsley or cilantro to the mix.

Nutritional Information:

Calories: 155, Protein: 3g, Carbohydrates: 29g, Fat: 3g, Fiber: 5g, Cholesterol: 0 mg, Sodium: 91 mg, Potassium: 497 mg

2 SERVINGS **5 MINUTES**

Directions:

1. Place the spinach, banana, pineapple, chia seeds, almond milk, ginger, and lemon juice into a blender. If you desire a touch of added sweetness, include the honey or agave syrup.
2. Blend on high until all the ingredients are thoroughly combined and the mixture reaches a smooth, creamy consistency. If needed, add more almond milk or coconut water to adjust the thickness to your preference.
3. Once blended to perfection, pour the detox smoothie into two glasses.
4. Serve immediately for maximum nutritional benefits and enjoy the revitalizing effects of this green powerhouse.

Celery Apple Cleanse

This refreshing and revitalizing Celery Apple Cleanse smoothie will help flush your body of toxins while replenishing essential nutrients. The crisp taste of celery combined with the sweetness of apple and the tang of lemon makes this not just a detox special but a tantalizing taste experience.

Equipment:

Blender, Knife, Cutting Board

Ingredients:

- 1 1/2 cup cold water
- 4 stalks organic celery, roughly chopped
- 1 large organic apple, cored and cut into chunks
- 1/2 organic cucumber, sliced
- Juice of 1/2 organic lemon
- 1 inch piece ginger, peeled
- A handful of fresh parsley
- A few mint leaves (optional for added freshness)
- Ice cubes (optional for a chilled beverage)

Tips:

You can strain the smoothie through cheesecloth or a fine mesh screen to get rid of any fibrous bits for an even smoother texture.

Nutritional Information:

Calories: 95, Protein: 1.5g, Carbohydrates: 24g, Fat: 0.5g, Fiber: 5g, Cholesterol: 0 mg, Sodium: 60 mg, Potassium: 412 mg

2 SERVINGS **10 MINUTES**

Directions:

1. Prepare all the fruits and vegetables by washing them thoroughly. Chop the celery, core and chop the apple, slice the cucumber, and peel the ginger.
2. Add the water and the chopped celery to the blender first and blend until smooth to ensure the fibrous stalks are thoroughly liquefied.
3. Then add the apple chunks, cucumber slices, lemon juice, and ginger into the blender.
4. Add parsley and mint leaves, if using, to the blend.
5. Place the lid on the blender and puree the mixture until it reaches a smooth consistency. If desired, add ice cubes to the blender to make a chilled smoothie.
6. Taste the smoothie and adjust the sweetness or tanginess as desired. You can adjust the smoothie's thickness by adding a little extra water.
7. Once blended to your liking, pour the detox smoothie into glasses and serve immediately.

Pineapple Parsley Pep

This invigorating, detoxifying smoothie boasts a vibrant blend of fresh pineapple and parsley, infusing your day with a burst of tropical flavor and potent nutrients. It's a perfect pick-me-up that combines the digestive benefits of pineapple with the detoxifying properties of parsley. A zesty touch of lemon and the natural sweetness of apple make this a tantalizing treat that's as delightful for the senses as it is beneficial for your body.

Equipment:

Blender, Measuring cups, Knife, Cutting board

Ingredients:

- 1 cup fresh pineapple, chopped
- 1/2 cup fresh parsley, stems removed
- 1 medium apple, cored and sliced
- Juice of 1 lemon
- 1 cup water or coconut water
- 1 tablespoon flax seeds (optional for added fiber)
- 1/2 inch piece of ginger, peeled (optional for a spicy kick)
- Ice cubes (optional for a colder smoothie)

Tips:

For an extra detoxifying effect, add a teaspoon of chlorella or spirulina powder to the blend. Ensure all fruits and parsley are thoroughly washed before use. Fresh ingredients always yield the best-tasting smoothie, but you can also use frozen pineapple if fresh is not available.

Nutritional Information:

Calories: 180, Protein: 2g, Carbohydrates: 40g, Fat: 1g, Fiber: 5g, Cholesterol: 0 mg, Sodium: 30 mg, Potassium: 270 mg

2 SERVINGS   5 MINUTES

Directions:

1. Prep all the fresh ingredients - chop the pineapple, remove parsley stems, core and slice the apple, and peel the ginger if you're using it.
2. In your blender, combine the chopped pineapple, fresh parsley, apple slices, lemon juice, water or coconut water, and optional flax seeds and ginger.
3. Blend on high until all the ingredients are well-combined and the mixture is smooth. You can add extra water or coconut water to the smoothie if it's too thick for you.
4. Taste and adjust the flavor as necessary. If you prefer a colder smoothie, blend in a few ice cubes until the desired temperature is reached.
5. Once everything is perfectly blended, pour the smoothie into two glasses.

Watermelon Basil Bliss

Dive into a refreshing, herbaceous escape with the Watermelon Basil Bliss. Perfect for detox and hydration, this smoothie combines the sweet summer taste of ripe watermelon with the aromatic twist of fresh basil. An ideal choice for warm days or when you're looking for a light drink to cleanse the palate and rejuvenate the senses.

Equipment:

Blender, Knife, Cutting Board

Ingredients:

- 2 cups seedless watermelon, cubed and preferably chilled
- 1/2 cup unsweetened coconut water
- 1/4 cup fresh basil leaves
- 1 tablespoon fresh lime juice
- 1 tablespoon chia seeds
- 6-8 ice cubes (optional, for a slushier texture)
- 1 teaspoon honey or agave syrup (optional, for added sweetness)

Tips:

For an even colder smoothie, freeze the watermelon cubes before blending. This will chill the drink without diluting it as the ice would.

Nutritional Information:

Calories: 100, Protein: 2g, Carbohydrates: 20g, Fat: 2g, Fiber: 3g, Cholesterol: 0 mg, Sodium: 25 mg, Potassium: 300 mg

2 SERVINGS **0 MINUTES**

Directions:

1. Place the cubed watermelon, coconut water, fresh basil leaves, lime juice, and chia seeds into the blender. If using, add the honey or agave syrup for sweetness.
2. Process the liquid at a high speed until it becomes smooth and the basil leaves are thoroughly blended in.
3. If a slushier consistency is desired, add the ice cubes and blend again until smooth.
4. Pour the smoothie into glasses and garnish with a sprig of basil if desired.
5. Serve immediately and enjoy your Watermelon Basil Bliss!

Smoothies for Weight Loss

Berry Metabolism Booster

Rev up your metabolism with this vibrant, nutrient-packed smoothie. Perfect for breakfast or a midday energy boost, the Berry Metabolism Booster combines succulent berries and protein-rich ingredients to help keep you feeling full and energized throughout the day.

Equipment:
Blender, Measuring Cups, Measuring Spoons

Ingredients:
- One cup of frozen mixed berries (strawberries, raspberries, and blueberries)
- 1/2 medium ripe banana
- 3/4 cup unsweetened almond milk
- 1/2 cup Greek yogurt, plain
- 1 tablespoon chia seeds
- One tablespoon of honey, or more to taste (for sweetness, optional)
- 2 teaspoons lemon juice
- A little amount of cayenne pepper (optional for increasing metabolism)
- Ice cubes (optional, depending on desired thickness)

Tips:
For an extra boost of metabolism-friendly ingredients, consider adding a scoop of your favorite protein powder or a handful of spinach to the smoothie before blending. The added greens will provide additional fiber and nutrients without significantly altering the taste.

Nutritional Information:
Calories: 160, Protein: 8g, Carbohydrates: 24g, Fat: 4g, Fiber: 5g, Cholesterol: 5mg, Sodium: 80mg, Potassium: 300mg

2 SERVINGS **5 MINUTES**

Directions:
1. Place the frozen berries, ripe banana, unsweetened almond milk, and Greek yogurt in the blender.
2. Add chia seeds, honey (if using), lemon juice, and a pinch of cayenne pepper to the mixture.
3. Blend until all the ingredients are well combined and smooth, adding ice cubes if necessary to reach your preferred consistency.
4. After tasting the smoothie, taste it again and add more honey if needed to make it more sweet.
5. Pour into two glasses and serve immediately for the freshest flavor and most potent metabolic impact.

Citrus Slimmer

Thrive on the tangy taste and slimming power of the Citrus Slimmer. This smoothie is crafted to enhance metabolism and aid in weight loss, while providing a refreshing zest that awakens the senses.

Equipment:

Blender, Measuring Cups, Knife

Ingredients:

- 1 cup Fresh Grapefruit Juice, no sugar added
- 1/2 Lemon, juiced
- 1/2 Lime, juiced
- 1 cup Spinach, fresh
- 1/2 cup Cucumber, peeled and sliced
- 1 tablespoon Chia Seeds
- 1/4 teaspoon Cayenne Pepper
- 1/2 cup Ice Cubes
- Stevia or honey to taste (optional)

Tips:

For an extra chill, you can freeze the grapefruit juice in an ice cube tray ahead of time and use these instead of regular ice cubes.

Nutritional Information:

Calories: 95, Protein: 2g, Carbohydrates: 18g, Fat: 1.5g, Fiber: 4g, Cholesterol: 0 mg, Sodium: 16 mg, Potassium: 300 mg

2 SERVINGS   10 MINUTES

Directions:

1. Combine grapefruit juice, lemon juice, lime juice, spinach, cucumber, chia seeds, and cayenne pepper in the blender.
2. Add ice cubes to the mix.
3. Process the ingredients at a high speed until it becomes creamy and smooth.
4. Taste and add a pinch of stevia or a drizzle of honey if a sweeter smoothie is desired.
5. If using sweetener, blend for an additional few seconds to incorporate it.
6. Pour into glasses and serve immediately for maximum freshness and benefit.

Kale and Apple Shred Smoothie

This vibrant green smoothie combines the powerful nutrient profile of kale with the sweet tartness of green apple, creating a deliciously refreshing drink that can help support your weight loss goals. High in fiber and antioxidants, this smoothie is not only nourishing but also aids in digestion and can kickstart your metabolism.

Equipment:

Blender, Knife, Cutting Board

Ingredients:

- Two cups of fresh kale with cut leaves and trimmed stems
- 1 medium green apple, cored and chopped
- 1 tablespoon chia seeds
- 1 tablespoon fresh lemon juice
- 1/2 cup unsweetened almond milk
- 1/2 cup water
- 1/2 cup ice cubes
- 1 teaspoon honey (optional)

Tips:

For a smoother texture, you can strain the smoothie through a fine-mesh sieve or use a high-powered blender. Consider adding a scoop of your preferred protein powder if you're seeking to increase your protein intake.

Nutritional Information:

Calories: 138, Protein: 4g, Carbohydrates: 27g, Fat: 3g, Fiber: 5g, Cholesterol: 0 mg, Sodium: 56 mg, Potassium: 448 mg

2 SERVINGS   10 MINUTES

Directions:

1. Add the kale, green apple, chia seeds, lemon juice, almond milk, and water into the blender.
2. Blend on high until the mixture is smooth and the kale is thoroughly processed.
3. Once the smoothie reaches the correct smoothness, add the ice cubes and combine once more.
4. Taste and if you prefer a bit of sweetness, add the teaspoon of honey and blend for a few seconds to incorporate.
5. Pour into glasses and serve immediately.

Banana Oat Balance

Find your equilibrium with this Banana Oat Balance smoothie, perfect for weight loss and full of wholesome ingredients to keep you full and satisfied. A blend of creamy bananas, hearty oats, and a hint of cinnamon, this smoothie is a great way to kick-start your day with a nutrient-packed, energizing drink.

Equipment:

Blender, Measuring Cups, Measuring Spoons

Ingredients:

- 2 Medium-sized ripe bananas, peeled
- 1/2 cup Rolled oats
- 1 cup Unsweetened almond milk
- 1/2 teaspoon Ground cinnamon
- 1 tablespoon Chia seeds
- 1 tablespoon Honey or maple syrup (optional, for sweetness)
- 4-6 Ice cubes

Tips:

For a colder smoothie, freeze the bananas in advance. For a more substantial beverage, you can up the protein level by adding a scoop of your preferred protein powder.

Nutritional Information:

Calories: 245, Protein: 5g, Carbohydrates: 47g, Fat: 4g, Fiber: 7g, Cholesterol: 0 mg, Sodium: 80 mg, Potassium: 422 mg

2 SERVINGS   **5 MINUTES**

Directions:

1. Place the rolled oats into the blender and blend for a few seconds to create a fine oat flour.
2. Add the bananas, almond milk, ground cinnamon, chia seeds, honey (if using), and ice cubes to the blender with the oat flour.
3. Make sure the chia seeds and oats are thoroughly blended in the smoothie by blending it on high speed until it becomes creamy and smooth. This should take around 1-2 minutes.
4. Taste and adjust sweetness if necessary, adding a little more honey or maple syrup if desired.
5. Pour into glasses and serve immediately for the freshest flavor and best texture.

Cinnamon Almond Swirl

Indulge in this creamy and nourishing Cinnamon Almond Swirl smoothie for a weight loss-friendly treat. Packed with protein and fiber to keep you full, it's sprinkled with warming cinnamon to rev up your metabolism and boasts a touch of natural sweetness that will satisfy any dessert cravings without the guilt.

Equipment:
Blender, Measuring Cups, Measuring Spoons

Ingredients:
- 1 cup unsweetened almond milk
- 1/2 cup Greek yogurt, plain, nonfat
- 2 tbsp almond butter, natural
- 1 medium banana, frozen and sliced
- 1 scoop vanilla protein powder (optional for added protein)
- 1/4 tsp cinnamon, ground, plus extra for garnish
- 1 tsp honey (adjust to taste; optional)
- 4-5 ice cubes (optional for thicker consistency)

Tips:
For added texture and nutrition, sprinkle some chia seeds or flaxseed on top of the smoothie before serving. If you prefer a nut-free version, substitute almond milk with oat milk and almond butter with sunflower seed butter.

Nutritional Information:
Calories: 235, Protein: 14g, Carbohydrates: 26g, Fat: 10g, Fiber: 4g, Cholesterol: 5 mg, Sodium: 180 mg, Potassium: 450 mg

2 SERVINGS 0 MINUTES

Directions:
1. Place the almond milk, Greek yogurt, almond butter, frozen banana slices, protein powder (if using), cinnamon, honey, and ice cubes into the blender.
2. Blend on high until the mixture is smooth and creamy, ensuring the ice is completely crushed and ingredients are well combined.
3. If needed, taste and add a bit more honey to regulate the sweetness.
4. Pour into two glasses and sprinkle with a pinch of cinnamon on top for an extra swirl of flavor.
5. Serve immediately and enjoy your Cinnamon Almond Swirl smoothie.

Grapefruit and Spinach Trim

This Grapefruit and Spinach Trim smoothie is a vibrant and invigorating blend that invigorates the palate and kick-starts your metabolism. High in fiber and low in calories, this refreshing smoothie is perfect for those looking to shed a few pounds while enjoying a tantalizing mix of tangy and earthy flavors.

Equipment:

Blender, Knife, Cutting Board

Ingredients:

- 1 large Red Grapefruit, peeled and seeds removed
- 2 cups Fresh Spinach
- 1/2 cup Unsweetened Almond Milk
- 1 tablespoon Chia Seeds
- 1/4 teaspoon Ground Cinnamon
- Ice cubes (optional, for a colder smoothie)
- Stevia or Honey (optional, for added sweetness)

Tips:

Ensure all the white pith from the grapefruit is removed as it can add a bitter taste to your smoothie. You may also try adding a scoop of your preferred plant-based protein powder for an added protein boost.

Nutritional Information:

Calories: 144, Protein: 3g, Carbohydrates: 25g, Fat: 4g, Fiber: 7g, Cholesterol: 0mg, Sodium: 91mg, Potassium: 447mg

2 SERVINGS

5 MINUTES

Directions:

1. Begin by preparing the grapefruit. Use a sharp knife on a cutting board to peel the grapefruit and remove any seeds. Make sure to retain as much of the juice as possible.
2. In the blender, combine the peeled grapefruit, fresh spinach, and unsweetened almond milk.
3. Add chia seeds and ground cinnamon to the mixture. Stir in a couple of ice cubes for a cooler smoothie.
4. Process at a high speed until the ingredients are well combined and the smoothie has a uniformly smooth texture.
5. Taste the smoothie, and if desired, sweeten with a touch of Stevia or honey to your liking. Blend again briefly to mix through the sweetener.
6. Pour the Grapefruit and Spinach Trim smoothie into glasses and serve immediately for the best flavor and nutrient retention.

Carrot and Orange Essence

Kick-start your day with this vibrant Carrot and Orange Essence smoothie. Packed with vitamin C, beta-carotene, and fiber, it's a refreshing weight loss ally that satiates and revitalizes in just a few sips. Perfect for morning nourishment or a mid-day energy boost.

Equipment:
Blender, Measuring Cups, Knife

Ingredients:
- 1 cup freshly squeezed orange juice
- 1 medium carrot, peeled and sliced
- 1/2 medium banana, frozen
- 1/2 cup unsweetened almond milk
- 1 tablespoon chia seeds
- A pinch of ground cinnamon
- 1/2 inch piece of fresh ginger, peeled
- Ice cubes (optional, for added chill)

Tips:
Add a scoop of your preferred vanilla or plain protein powder for an additional protein boost. If the smoothie seems too tart, you may naturally sweeten it with a small amount of honey or maple syrup.

Nutritional Information:
Calories: 150, Protein: 3g, Carbohydrates: 29g, Fat: 3g, Fiber: 5g, Cholesterol: 0 mg, Sodium: 80 mg, Potassium: 400 mg

2 SERVINGS **10 MINUTES**

Directions:
1. Combine the orange juice, sliced carrot, frozen banana, almond milk, and chia seeds in the blender.
2. Add the ground cinnamon and fresh ginger to bring a gentle warmth and spice to the mix.
3. If you prefer a colder drink, add a handful of ice cubes to the blender.
4. Blend on high until the mixture is smooth and the ingredients are thoroughly incorporated.
5. To suit your tastes, add a little extra orange juice or almond milk to the smoothie if it's too thick.
6. To ensure optimal flavor and nutrient retention, pour the smoothie into glasses and serve right away.

Green Tea Infusion

This Green Tea Infusion smoothie is a perfect blend of metabolism-boosting and antioxidant-rich ingredients, making it a great addition to any weight loss routine. The combination of green tea and fresh greens provides a refreshing and energizing drink that not only helps in shedding extra pounds but also supports overall health.

Equipment:

Blender, Measuring cups, Knife

Ingredients:

- 1 cup Brewed green tea, cooled
- 1 cup Baby spinach leaves
- 1/2 medium Cucumber, sliced
- 1 small Green apple, cored and chopped
- 1 tablespoon Chia seeds
- 1 tablespoon Fresh lemon juice
- 1/4 inch of freshly peeled and chopped ginger
- 1/2 cup Ice cubes
- Optional: 1 teaspoon Honey, or to taste (for those not strictly counting calories)

Tips:

To enhance the smoothie's fat-burning capabilities, drink it in the morning or before workouts when your metabolism is naturally higher. You can also use matcha powder in place of brewed green tea for an extra antioxidant boost.

Nutritional Information:

Calories: 70, Protein: 2g, Carbohydrates: 12g, Fat: 2g, Fiber: 4g, Cholesterol: 0 mg, Sodium: 16 mg, Potassium: 232 mg

2 SERVINGS **10 MINUTES**

Directions:

1. Begin by brewing green tea and allowing it to cool completely. This can be done ahead of time to speed up the process.
2. In your blender, combine the cooled green tea, baby spinach leaves, cucumber slices, chopped green apple, chia seeds, fresh lemon juice, and minced ginger.
3. Add the ice cubes to the mixture.
4. Blend on high until the smoothie is creamy and all the ingredients are well blended.
5. Taste the smoothie, and if you prefer it a little sweeter and aren't strictly counting calories, you can add honey to taste and then blend again.
6. Pour into glasses and enjoy immediately for the best flavor and nutrient retention.

Green Veggie Blends

Spinach Sunshine Sip

Dive into the zest of fresh greens with the Spinach Sunshine Sip—a jubilant blend of leafy spinach and tangy fruits that promises a radiant start to your day. This elixir offers a harmonious balance of nutrition and flavor, perfectly suited for health enthusiasts and smoothie lovers alike.

Equipment:

Blender, Measuring Spoons, Measuring Cups

Ingredients:

- 2 cups fresh spinach leaves
- 1 ripe banana
- 1/2 cup frozen pineapple chunks
- 1/2 cup frozen mango chunks
- 1/2 medium avocado
- 1 tablespoon chia seeds
- 1 cup unsweetened almond milk or water
- Juice of 1/2 lemon
- Optional: 1 tablespoon honey or agave syrup (for added sweetness)

Tips:

Save time in the morning by prepping your fruits and storing them in the freezer. Always ensure the blender lid is secure to avoid any spills. If you prefer a colder smoothie, use cold almond milk or add a few ice cubes to the mix before blending.

Nutritional Information:

Calories: 235, Protein: 4g, Carbohydrates: 35g, Fat: 10g, Fiber: 9g, Cholesterol: 0 mg, Sodium: 110 mg, Potassium: 688 mg

2 SERVINGS **10 MINUTES**

Directions:

1. Prepare the spinach by giving it a gentle rinse under cold water and then patting it dry with a paper towel.
2. Peel the banana and slice it into chunks. Pit and scoop out the avocado.
3. Add the spinach, banana, pineapple, mango, avocado, and chia seeds to the blender.
4. Pour in the almond milk or water for a smoother consistency, depending on your preference.
5. Squeeze in the fresh lemon juice for a bit of zest and tanginess to the mix.
6. Process all the ingredients at a high speed until they are creamy and smooth. To get the right consistency, thin out any thick spots in the smoothie by adding a small amount extra liquid.
7. Taste and blend in honey or agave syrup if a sweeter drink is desired.
8. Pour the smoothie into glasses and serve immediately for the freshest taste and the most nutritional benefit.

Kale Kickstart Fusion

Start your day with a burst of energy from the Kale Kickstart Fusion. This power-packed green smoothie combines kale's nutritional prowess with the tanginess of apple and the smooth, healthy fats from avocado, giving you the perfect blend to boost your morning routine.

Equipment:
Blender, Measuring Cups, Knife, Cutting Board

Ingredients:
- Two cups of chopped leaves and trimmed stems of Kale
- 1 medium Apple, cored and sliced
- 1/2 Avocado, pitted and scooped
- 1 tablespoon Chia Seeds
- One cup of plain almond milk, or any other plant-based milk
- 1/2 cup Greek yogurt without additional protein (optional).
- For sweetness, add one tablespoon of either honey or agave nectar.
- 1/2 cup Ice (if desired for a cooler drink)
- Juice of 1/2 Lemon

Tips:
For an extra health boost, try adding a scoop of your favorite protein powder. Ensure your apple and avocado are ripe for the best flavor and smoothest texture. Chia seeds not only enrich with omega-3 fatty acids but also help thicken your smoothie. If you prefer a colder smoothie, you can freeze your kale and apple slices beforehand.

Nutritional Information:
Calories: 235, Protein: 6g, Carbohydrates: 31g, Fat: 12g, Fiber: 6g, Cholesterol: 0 mg, Sodium: 110 mg, Potassium: 667 mg

2 SERVINGS **5 MINUTES**

Directions:
1. Place the kale, apple, avocado, and chia seeds into the blender.
2. Add the unsweetened almond milk and Greek yogurt, if using.
3. Squeeze in the juice of half a lemon to add a refreshing citrus note.
4. For a touch of sweetness, drizzle in honey or agave nectar if desired.
5. Finally, add ice to help chill and thicken your smoothie.
6. Using a high speed blender, blend everything until it's smooth and creamy, scraping down the sides as needed.
7. If the smoothie is too thick, add a bit more milk; if it's not sweet enough, add more honey. Taste the smoothie and adjust the ingredients as necessary.
8. Pour into two glasses and serve immediately for the freshest flavor and nutrient boost.

Celery Zing Twist

Awaken your senses with the Celery Zing Twist; a refreshing green veggie blend that's perfect for a nutrient-packed start to your day or a revitalizing afternoon pick-me-up. Experience the invigorating fusion of crisp celery and tangy citrus with a hint of ginger to spice things up.

Equipment:

Blender, Measuring Cups, Knife, Cutting Board

Ingredients:

- 3 large Celery stalks
- 1 medium Green apple, cored and chopped
- 1/2 cup Fresh spinach leaves
- 1/2 small Cucumber, sliced
- 1 Tbsp Fresh ginger root, grated
- 1 Tbsp Fresh parsley leaves
- 1 cup Unsweetened almond milk
- Juice of 1/2 Lemon
- Juice of 1/2 Lime
- Optional: 1 tsp Chia seeds or flaxseeds for an omega-3 boost
- Add a pinch of cayenne pepper for added spiciness if desired.

Tips:

If you prefer a colder smoothie, you can chill the ingredients beforehand or add a few ice cubes to the blender before mixing. Additionally, if you like your smoothies on the sweeter side, consider adding a small amount of honey or agave nectar.

Nutritional Information:

Calories: 95, Protein: 3g, Carbohydrates: 20g, Fat: 1g, Fiber: 5g, Cholesterol: 0 mg, Sodium: 125 mg, Potassium: 397 mg

2 SERVINGS | **10 MINUTES**

Directions:

1. Make sure to give every fruit and vegetable a thorough wash to get rid of any dirt or residue.
2. Chop the celery, green apple, and cucumber into pieces that are small enough to blend easily.
3. Grate the ginger root until you have the needed amount.
4. Add the celery, green apple, spinach, cucumber, ginger, and parsley into the blender.
5. Pour in the unsweetened almond milk.
6. Squeeze in the juice from the lemon and lime.
7. If desired, add chia seeds or flaxseeds and/or a dash of cayenne pepper.
8. Blend on high until completely smooth and well combined, approximately 45 seconds to 1 minute. To get the right consistency, you can add a little extra almond milk if the smoothie is too thick.
9. Taste and adjust the seasoning, adding more lemon or lime juice if needed for additional zing.
10. Serve immediately for the freshest taste and the most nutritional benefits.

Garden Greens Smoothie

This Garden Greens Smoothie is a fresh and vibrant drink packed full of nourishing ingredients, perfect for kick-starting your day or re-energizing your afternoon. With a blend of leafy greens and creamy avocado, this smoothie doesn't just taste great – it's also a powerhouse of nutrients.

Equipment:

Blender, Measuring Cups, Knife

Ingredients:

- 1 cup fresh spinach leaves
- 1/2 cup kale leaves, stems removed
- 1 medium ripe avocado, pitted and scooped
- 1/2 medium cucumber, sliced
- 2 celery stalks, chopped
- 1 green apple, cored and sliced
- 1 tablespoon fresh parsley leaves
- 1/2 tablespoon fresh ginger, grated
- Juice of 1 lemon
- 1 1/2 cups cold water or coconut water
- 6 ice cubes (optional)
- 1 tablespoon chia seeds (optional)

Tips:

For an eye-catching display, top your smoothie with a slice of lemon or a sprig of parsley. You can add a scoop of your preferred protein powder or a handful of nuts, such as cashews or almonds, for an added protein boost.

Nutritional Information:

Calories: 180, Protein: 4g, Carbohydrates: 27g, Fat: 8g, Fiber: 9g, Cholesterol: 0 mg, Sodium: 60 mg, Potassium: 879 mg

2 SERVINGS | **10 MINUTES**

Directions:

1. Place the spinach, kale, avocado, cucumber, celery, apple, parsley, and ginger into the blender.
2. After adding the coconut water or cold water, squeeze in the lemon juice.
3. If you prefer a colder smoothie, add the ice cubes to the mixture.
4. Blend on high speed until all the ingredients are completely smooth. Depending on your blender, this might take 1 to 2 minutes.
5. If the smoothie is thicker than you like, adjust the consistency by adding a little more water or coconut water and blend again.
6. Sprinkle in the chia seeds and pulse a few times to incorporate them into the smoothie for an added dose of fiber and omega-3 fatty acids.

Peppy Parsley Potion

Dive into a garden-fresh experience with the Peppy Parsley Potion, a vibrant green veggie smoothie that invigorates the senses and packs a punch of rich nutrients. This fragrant blend combines the fresh, herbaceous notes of parsley with the creamy texture of banana and the subtle heat of ginger, making it an ideal pick-me-up for any time of day.

Equipment:

Blender, Measuring Cups, Knife

Ingredients:

- 1 cup packed fresh parsley leaves
- 1 ripe banana
- 1/2 cup fresh spinach leaves
- 1 small cucumber, roughly chopped
- 1 inch piece fresh ginger, peeled and grated
- Juice of 1 lemon
- 1 tablespoon chia seeds
- 1 cup unsweetened almond milk
- Ice cubes (optional, for a chilled smoothie)

Tips:

For a nutritional boost, add a scoop of your favorite green superfood powder. To ensure the smoothie is extra smooth, blend the parsley and liquids first before adding the remaining ingredients.

Nutritional Information:

Calories: 157, Protein: 4g, Carbohydrates: 27g, Fat: 4g, Fiber: 6g, Cholesterol: 0 mg, Sodium: 110 mg, Potassium: 499 mg

2 SERVINGS   **10 MINUTES**

Directions:

1. Wash the parsley, spinach, and cucumber thoroughly. Peel the banana, and grate the ginger.
2. Place the parsley, banana, spinach, cucumber, grated ginger, lemon juice, chia seeds, and almond milk into the blender.
3. If a cold smoothie is preferred, add a handful of ice cubes.
4. Process the ingredients at a high speed until it becomes creamy and smooth. To get the right consistency, you can add a little extra almond milk if the smoothie is too thick.
5. Taste and adjust the flavor as needed, adding more lemon juice for zest or ginger for spice.
6. Pour into glasses and serve immediately.

Crisp Cucumber Cooler

Indulge in the refreshing zest of the Crisp Cucumber Cooler, a perfect blend of garden-fresh veggies with a hint of mint. This vibrant green concoction is ideal for a morning boost or a midday pick-me-up.

Equipment:

Blender, Measuring Cups, Knife, Cutting Board

Ingredients:

- 1 large cucumber, peeled and sliced
- 1 cup baby spinach leaves
- 1/2 ripe avocado
- 1 tablespoon fresh mint leaves
- 1 cup coconut water
- 1 tablespoon lemon juice
- 1 tablespoon chia seeds (optional)
- 1/2 cup ice cubes
- Honey or agave syrup to taste (optional)

Tips:

For an extra protein kick, add a scoop of your preferred neutral-tasting protein powder. Keep your cooler chilled longer by serving it in pre-chilled glasses.

Nutritional Information:

Calories: 104, Protein: 2g, Carbohydrates: 14g, Fat: 5g, Fiber: 5g, Cholesterol: 0 mg, Sodium: 132 mg, Potassium: 593 mg

2 SERVINGS **10 MINUTES**

Directions:

1. Wash all the vegetables and mint leaves thoroughly.
2. Cut the cucumber into slices and the avocado in half, removing the pit.
3. Place the cucumber, spinach, avocado, mint leaves, and ice cubes into your blender.
4. Stir in the lemon juice and coconut water.
5. If you want a touch of sweetness, add honey or agave syrup to your preference.
6. Process the mixture at high speed until it becomes creamy and smooth. Pause to scrape down the sides if needed.
7. Taste the smoothie, and adjust sweetness or add more coconut water if it's too thick.
8. Sprinkle in the chia seeds and blend for an additional 30 seconds if a richer source of fiber is desired.
9. For optimal flavor and nutrition, immediately pour into glasses and enjoy.

Basil & Spinach Refresher

Dive into a garden-fresh, nutrient-packed green smoothie that energizes your day with vibrant flavors. The Basil & Spinach Refresher offers a harmonious blend of leafy greens, zesty citrus, and a hint of sweetness that will awaken your senses and rejuvenate your spirit.

Equipment:

Blender, Measuring cups and spoons

Ingredients:

- 2 cups fresh spinach leaves, packed
- 1/2 cup fresh basil leaves, packed
- 1 ripe banana, peeled and frozen
- 1/2 cup cucumber, peeled and sliced
- 1 tablespoon chia seeds
- Juice of 1 lemon
- 1 cup coconut water or plain water
- One tablespoon of agave syrup or honey (optional; adds sweetness)
- For a cooler smoothie, add optional ice cubes.

Tips:

For an extra protein punch, add a scoop of your favorite plant-based protein powder before blending. To ensure a cold smoothie without diluting it with ice, make sure the banana is well frozen before use.

Nutritional Information:

Calories: 140, Protein: 3g, Carbohydrates: 27g, Fat: 3g, Fiber: 5g, Cholesterol: 0 mg, Sodium: 60 mg, Potassium: 540 mg

2 SERVINGS   **5 MINUTES**

Directions:

1. Place the spinach, basil, banana, cucumber, chia seeds, and lemon juice into the blender.
2. Add the coconut water to ease blending. If you desire a sweeter taste, include the tablespoon of honey or agave syrup.
3. Process the smoothie at a high speed until it has a creamy, smooth consistency. If the mixture is too thick, add a little more water to achieve your desired texture.
4. Taste and add ice cubes if you prefer a colder beverage. Blend again briefly after adding ice.
5. Pour into two glasses and serve immediately, garnished with a sprig of basil if desired.

Romaine Calm & Blend On

Savor the refreshing blend of hearty greens and a touch of sweet fruit in this nutrient-packed green smoothie. It's the perfect pick-me-up to start your day or to enjoy as a mid-afternoon snack. Gentle on the palate with a hint of zesty lemon, this smoothie is as calming as it is invigorating.

Equipment:

Blender, Measuring cups, Knife

Ingredients:

- 2 cups chopped romaine lettuce
- 1 cup fresh spinach leaves
- 1 medium ripe banana, sliced
- 1/2 cup cucumber, chopped
- 1 medium apple, cored and sliced
- Juice of 1 lemon
- 1 tablespoon chia seeds
- 1 cup coconut water (or water for a less sweet option)
- 6 to 8 ice cubes
- Fresh mint leaves for garnish (optional)

Tips:

To ensure a smooth drink, start by blending the greens and liquid before adding the other ingredients. Also, freezing the banana ahead of time can eliminate the need for ice and make your smoothie even creamier.

Nutritional Information:

Calories: 180, Protein: 3g, Carbohydrates: 39g, Fat: 2g, Fiber: 7g, Cholesterol: 0 mg, Sodium: 87 mg, Potassium: 740 mg

2 SERVINGS

5 MINUTES

Directions:

1. Place the chopped romaine lettuce and spinach leaves into the blender.
2. Add the sliced banana, chopped cucumber, and sliced apple to the greens.
3. Juice one lemon, being careful not to get any seeds in the mixer.
4. Sprinkle the chia seeds over the fruit and vegetables for an added nutrient boost.
5. Pour in the coconut water to help the ingredients blend smoothly. If you prefer a thinner consistency, you might add a bit more as you blend.
6. To give your smoothie a cool, refreshing taste, add some ice cubes.
7. Blend on high until the smoothie has the required consistency and all the ingredients are well blended. If needed, stop the blender and stir the mixture before continuing to blend.
8. Transfer the smoothie into glasses, top with a fresh mint sprig if preferred, and serve right away.

Post-Workout Power Blends

Protein Power-Up

Your muscles are craving protein to help them develop and heal after a strenuous workout. Our "Protein Power-Up" smoothie is a deliciously creamy blend rich in high-quality protein and essential micronutrients to aid in your muscle recovery and satiety. Its natural sweetness and smooth texture will satisfy your taste buds and power you through post-exercise recovery.

Equipment:
Blender, Measuring Cups, Measuring Spoons

Ingredients:
- 1 scoop (approximately 30g) Vanilla Whey Protein Powder
- 1 medium Banana, sliced and frozen
- One cup of unsweetened almond milk (or your preferred milk)
- Two teaspoons of natural peanut butter or almond butter
- 1/2 cup Greek Yogurt, plain
- 1 tablespoon Chia Seeds
- 1 tablespoon Honey (optional for added sweetness)
- 1/4 teaspoon Cinnamon (optional for flavor)
- Ice Cubes (optional, for a thicker texture)

Tips:
Make sure your banana is frozen beforehand to give your smoothie an ice-cream-like thickness without diluting the flavor. You can prepare and freeze banana slices in advance to save time.

Nutritional Information:
Calories: 325, Protein: 28g, Carbohydrates: 23g, Fat: 15g, Fiber: 5g, Cholesterol: 10 mg, Sodium: 200 mg, Potassium: 450 mg

2 SERVINGS   **5 MINUTES**

Directions:
1. Place the frozen banana slices, whey protein powder, natural peanut or almond butter, unsweetened almond milk, and Greek yogurt into the blender.
2. To increase the amount of fiber and omega-3 fatty acids in the mixture, add chia seeds.
3. For added sweetness or a hint of spice, consider adding honey and cinnamon to the mix.
4. Blend on high until the ingredients are well combined and the texture is smooth. To get the right consistency, you can add a little extra almond milk if the smoothie is too thick. For an even frostier treat, toss in a few ice cubes before blending.
5. To ensure optimal freshness and strength, promptly serve the smoothie by pouring it into two glasses.

Banana-Peanut Punch

This energizing Banana-Peanut Punch is a sublime blend of nutty richness and smooth, sweet banana, making it an ideal choice for refueling post-workout. With a foundation of protein-packed peanut butter and potassium-rich bananas, you'll have the perfect balance of nutrients to support muscle recovery and a swift energy boost.

Equipment:

Blender, Measuring Cups, Measuring Spoons

Ingredients:

- 2 Medium-sized ripe bananas
- 2 Tbsp Unsweetened peanut butter
- 1 Cup Low-fat milk or plant-based milk (such as almond, soy, or oat)
- 1/2 Cup Greek yogurt or plant-based alternative
- 1 Tbsp Honey (optional, for added sweetness)
- 1/2 Tsp Vanilla extract
- 1 Cup Ice cubes (add more for a thicker smoothie)
- One scoop of vanilla or plain protein powder (additional protein optional)

Tips:

For an extra boost of energy and texture, you can add a tablespoon of rolled oats before blending. If you prefer a vegan version, ensure your protein powder is plant-based and use a dairy-free yogurt and milk alternative. Customize the thickness by adjusting the amount of ice or milk.

Nutritional Information:

Calories: 345, Protein: 16g, Carbohydrates: 41g, Fat: 16g, Fiber: 5g, Cholesterol: 30 mg, Sodium: 150 mg, Potassium: 622 mg

2 SERVINGS   **5 MINUTES**

Directions:

1. Peel the bananas and place them into the blender.
2. Add the peanut butter, milk, Greek yogurt, honey (if using), vanilla extract, and protein powder (if using) to the blender.
3. Top off with ice cubes.
4. Blend on high speed until all ingredients are smoothly combined and the texture is creamy.
5. To ensure optimal flavor and nutrient retention, pour the smoothie into two glasses and serve right away.

Muscle Recovery Mix

After a tough workout, replenish your body with this blend of high-protein yogurt, potassium-rich banana, antioxidants from mixed berries, and a touch of natural sweetness, designed to aid muscle recovery and rehydration.

Equipment:

Blender, Measuring cups, Measuring spoons

Ingredients:

- 1 cup Greek yogurt (plain or vanilla)
- 1 medium banana
- 1/2 cup mixed berries (blueberries, strawberries, raspberries)
- 1 tablespoon almond butter
- 1 teaspoon chia seeds
- 1 cup spinach (fresh or frozen)
- half a cup of either regular or coconut water
- 1 scoop protein powder (optional)
- Ice cubes (optional for a thicker consistency)

Tips:

For an extra cooling effect, freeze your banana and berries in advance. You can also personalize this smoothie with other recovery-aiding ingredients like a teaspoon of turmeric or a tablespoon of hemp seeds.

Nutritional Information:

Calories: 245, Protein: 19g, Carbohydrates: 36g, Fat: 6g, Fiber: 5g, Cholesterol: 10 mg, Sodium: 61 mg, Potassium: 532 mg"

2 SERVINGS **5 MINUTES**

Directions:

1. Place the Greek yogurt, banana, mixed berries, almond butter, chia seeds, spinach, and coconut water into the blender.
2. Add in the optional protein powder if desired for an extra protein boost.
3. Add a handful of ice cubes if a thicker smoothie is preferred.
4. Process at high speed until smooth and creamy, stopping occasionally to scrape down the edges.
5. To ensure optimal freshness and effectiveness, pour the smoothie into two glasses and serve right away.

Berry Blast Recharge

Looking for a tasty way to recharge after a workout? Say hello to the Berry Blast Recharge! This smoothie is a delicious combination of berries and protein – perfect for muscle recovery and refueling your energy stores. The antioxidants from the mixed berries paired with the creaminess of Greek yogurt will ensure your post-workout treat is both nutritious and satisfying.

Equipment:

Blender, Measuring Cups, Measuring Spoons

Ingredients:

- One medium banana;
- One cup of frozen mixed berries (strawberries, raspberries, and blueberries)
- Half a cup of plain or vanilla Greek yogurt for added taste;
- One cup of unsweetened almond milk (or any other plant-based milk of your choosing)
- 1 scoop Vanilla or Berry Flavored Protein Powder
- 1 tablespoon Chia Seeds
- 1 tablespoon Honey (or to taste, optional)
- Ice Cubes (optional, for a thicker consistency)

Tips:

A handful of fresh spinach or kale can be added to the mixture to increase the antioxidant content even further; this won't significantly change the taste and will have extra health advantages. If you want a smoothie that is sweeter without using honey, consider adding a pitted Medjool date to the mixture before blending.

Nutritional Information:

Calories: 280, Protein: 20g, Carbohydrates: 35g, Fat: 6g, Fiber: 7g, Cholesterol: 5 mg, Sodium: 95 mg, Potassium: 520 mg

2 SERVINGS   5 MINUTES

Directions:

1. Place the frozen mixed berries, banana, Greek yogurt, almond milk, protein powder, chia seeds, and honey into the blender.
2. Process the mixture on high until it becomes creamy and smooth. You can adjust the smoothie's consistency by adding extra almond milk if it's too thick.
3. If you desire a colder and thicker smoothie, add a few ice cubes to the mixture and blend again until smooth.
4. Smoothie into two glasses and serve right away for optimal flavor and nutritional value.

Choco-Nut Energy Boost

Unleash the delight of a guilt-free post-workout indulgence with this rich and creamy Choco-Nut Energy Boost smoothie. Packed with high-quality protein, healthy fats, and replenishing carbohydrates, it's the perfect beverage to support muscle recovery and satisfy your chocolate cravings after a strenuous workout.

Equipment:

Blender, Measuring Cups, Measuring Spoons

Ingredients:

- 1 cup Almond milk (unsweetened)
- 1 medium Banana (frozen)
- 2 tbsp Peanut butter (natural, without added sugar)
- 1 tbsp Cocoa powder (unsweetened)
- 1 scoop Whey protein powder (chocolate flavored)
- 1 tbsp Chia seeds
- 1 tbsp Honey (optional, for added sweetness)
- 4-5 Ice cubes (optional, for added thickness)

Tips:

For an extra nutritional punch, sprinkle a few cacao nibs or add a handful of spinach to the blend for added antioxidants and iron. If you have a peanut allergy, feel free to use almond butter or any other nut or seed butter of your choosing in its place.

Nutritional Information:

Calories: 325, Protein: 20g, Carbohydrates: 25g, Fat: 16g, Fiber: 6g, Cholesterol: 30 mg, Sodium: 200 mg, Potassium: 400 mg

2 SERVINGS   5 MINUTES

Directions:

1. Place the almond milk, frozen banana, peanut butter, cocoa powder, chocolate-flavored whey protein powder, chia seeds, and honey (if using), into the blender.
2. Blend on high speed until all components are fully combined and the texture is smooth and creamy. If the mixture is too thick, add more almond milk to reach the desired consistency.
3. Add ice cubes if a thicker, frostier texture is preferred, and blend again until smooth.
4. After dividing the smoothie between two glasses, serve right away.

Tropical Refuel Shake

Designed to replenish and invigorate the body after a vigorous exercise session, the "Tropical Refuel Shake" is a creamy, rich, and delectable smoothie. Its selection of tropical fruits and protein-rich ingredients provides an enjoyable way to aid muscle recovery and rehydration. Enjoy this flavorful concoction that takes your taste buds on a mini vacation while helping your body bounce back faster.

Equipment:

Blender, Measuring Cups, Measuring Spoons

Ingredients:

- 1 cup coconut water
- 1/2 cup Greek yogurt, plain
- 1 scoop vanilla or plain protein powder
- 1 medium banana, frozen
- 1/2 cup pineapple chunks, frozen
- 1/2 cup mango chunks, frozen
- 1 tablespoon chia seeds
- 1/2 teaspoon turmeric powder (optional for an anti-inflammatory boost)
- Ice cubes (optional, for a thicker consistency)
- A sprig of mint or a slice of lime, for garnish (optional)

Tips:

For an extra dose of electrolytes, replace coconut water with an equal amount of coconut milk and a small pinch of sea salt. Freeze your fresh bananas and pineapple chunks in advance to ensure the smoothie has a solid, milkshake-like consistency.

Nutritional Information:

Calories: 235, Protein: 20g, Carbohydrates: 35g, Fat: 3g, Fiber: 5g, Cholesterol: 10 mg, Sodium: 167 mg, Potassium: 700 mg

2 SERVINGS **0 MINUTES**

Directions:

1. Place the coconut water, Greek yogurt, and protein powder in the blender as the base to ensure smooth blending.
2. Add the frozen banana, pineapple, and mango chunks on top of the liquid.
3. Sprinkle in the chia seeds and turmeric powder, if using.
4. Blend all the ingredients on high speed until smooth, creamy, and well combined, adding ice cubes if desired for a thicker texture.
5. Taste and add a touch more coconut water if the shake is too thick, or a few more frozen chunks if too thin.
6. Transfer the smoothie between two glasses and decorate with a lime slice or a sprig of mint, if preferred.

Sweet Spinach Stamina

Pack a punch into your post-workout routine with this nutrient-dense, muscle-replenishing Sweet Spinach Stamina smoothie. Brimming with fresh greens, energizing fruits, and a hint of sweetness, this is your go-to drink for quick recovery and sustained energy. This vibrant blend strikes the perfect balance between nourishment and flavor, ensuring your body gets what it needs while your taste buds dance with delight.

Equipment:
Blender, Measuring Cups and Spoons

Ingredients:
- 2 cups Fresh Spinach Leaves
- 1 medium-sized Ripe Banana
- 1/2 cup Greek Yogurt (plain or vanilla for added sweetness)
- 1 tablespoon Honey or Agave Syrup
- 1 tablespoon Almond Butter
- Half a cup of almond milk (or any other kind of milk, without sugar added)
- 1 scoop Vanilla or Unflavored Protein Powder
- 1/2 cup Frozen Pineapple Chunks
- 1/2 teaspoon Chia Seeds (optional)
- Ice cubes (optional, depending on desired thickness)

Tips:
For an extra cooling effect, use a frozen banana. For additional sweetness without added sugars, consider adding a few drops of stevia or a pinch of cinnamon. Customize your smoothie by adding other preferred superfoods such as flaxseeds or a handful of kale.

Nutritional Information:
Calories: 295, Protein: 19g, Carbohydrates: 39g, Fat: 8g, Fiber: 4g, Cholesterol: 5 mg, Sodium: 125 mg, Potassium: 620 mg

2 SERVINGS **10 MINUTES**

Directions:
1. Place the fresh spinach leaves into your blender, packing them down if necessary.
2. Add the ripe banana, Greek yogurt, honey, almond butter, almond milk, and protein powder on top of the spinach.
3. Toss in the frozen pineapple chunks and chia seeds if using.
4. Blend on high until all the ingredients are well combined and the mixture is smooth. You can adjust the smoothie's consistency by adding extra almond milk if it's too thick. If you want your smoothie to be thicker and colder, add more ice cubes.
5. For optimal post-workout effects, pour the smoothie into two glasses and enjoy right away.

Almond-Date Dynamo

Crafted to refuel your body post-workout, the Almond-Date Dynamo is a creamy blend rich in protein and natural sugars for a quick energy boost. Almond butter provides heart-healthy monounsaturated fats, while dates offer a hit of potassium to support muscle recovery. The subtle, earthy spice of cinnamon complements the sweetness and rounds out this nutritious indulgence.

Equipment:

Blender

Ingredients:

- 1 1/2 cups Almond Milk (unsweetened)
- 2 tbsp Almond Butter (natural, no added salt or sugar)
- 4 Medjool Dates (pitted)
- 1 frozen Banana (medium size, sliced)
- 1 scoop Vanilla Protein Powder (plant-based for a vegan option)
- 1/2 tsp Ground Cinnamon
- 1/2 cup Ice Cubes
- Optional: 1 tsp Chia Seeds (for an omega-3 boost)

Tips:

If you don't have fresh bananas on hand, frozen bananas work just as well and provide an extra creamy texture to the smoothie. Soak the dates in warm water for a few minutes before blending if they feel too firm. This will help them blend more easily and provide a smoother consistency.

Nutritional Information:

Calories: 345, Protein: 20g, Carbohydrates: 46g, Fat: 11g, Fiber: 7g, Cholesterol: 0 mg, Sodium: 190 mg, Potassium: 674 mg

2 SERVINGS   5 MINUTES

Directions:

1. Add all the ingredients, starting with the almond milk, to the blender to facilitate better blending.
2. Blend on high until smooth and creamy, ensuring the dates and ice are well-incorporated, which should take about 1-2 minutes.
3. If the smoothie is too thick, add a splash more almond milk and blend again to reach your desired consistency.
4. Transfer into glasses and garnish with a pinch of chia seeds or cinnamon, if preferred.

Conclusion

Thank you for joining us on this delicious journey through the world of smoothies. We hope that this book has provided you with the inspiration, knowledge, and tools needed to create a variety of nutritious and flavorful smoothies that cater to your health goals and taste preferences.

Smoothies are a versatile and enjoyable way to incorporate more fruits, vegetables, and other nutrient-dense ingredients into your diet. By experimenting with the recipes and tips provided, you can find the perfect blends that not only delight your taste buds but also nourish your body. Remember, the key to a great smoothie lies in using fresh, high-quality ingredients and a good blender to achieve that perfect consistency.

As you continue to explore and create your own smoothie recipes, we encourage you to have fun and be adventurous with your ingredient choices. Don't hesitate to adjust and modify the recipes to suit your personal needs and preferences. The possibilities are endless, and the benefits to your health and well-being are significant.

We would love to hear about your experiences and feedback. Your insights and suggestions are invaluable to us and help us improve and provide even better content in the future. If you enjoyed this book and found it helpful, **please consider leaving a review on Amazon**. Your feedback not only supports us but also helps other readers discover the joy and benefits of smoothie making.

Thank you once again for choosing the **"Smoothie Recipe Book."** Here's to blending your way to a healthier, happier you! Enjoy your smoothies, and don't forget to share your favorite creations with friends and family.

Happy blending!

Index

A
Almond-Date Dynamo 84
Apple Cider Vinegar Revive 51
Apple Orchard Adventure 35
Apple Pie Energizer 18
Autumn Pumpkin Patch Smoothie 25
Avocado Toast Smoothie 21

B
Banana Nut Morning 17
Banana Oat Balance 62
Banana-Peanut Punch 78
Basil & Spinach Refresher 74
Berry Blast Recharge 80
Berry Cherry Jubilee Smoothie 30
Berry Metabolism Booster 59

C
Carrot Citrus Purge 53
Carrot and Orange Essence 65
Celery Apple Cleanse 55
Celery Zing Twist 70
Cherry Almond Boost 20
Chia Seed Citrus Fusion 47
Choco-Nut Energy Boost 81
Cinnamon Almond Swirl 63
Cinnamon Apple Balance 42
Citrus Slimmer 60
Coco-Cucumber Cooler 48
Cozy Pear Ginger Blend 29
Creamy Avocado Dream 43
Crisp Cucumber Cooler 73
Cucumber Mint Refresher 52

G
Garden Greens Smoothie 71
Ginger Peach Soothe 44
Grapefruit and Spinach Trim 64
Green Monster Mystery 38
Green Tea Infusion 66

H
Harvest Apple Cinnamon Swirl 27

Hidden Veggie Chocolate Surprise 34

K
Kale Kickstart Fusion 69
Kale and Apple Shred Smoothie 61
Kale and Blueberry Burst 46

L
Lemon Ginger Zest 50
Low-Sugar Berry Bliss 41

M
Morning Berry Awakening 14
Muscle Recovery Mix 79

O
Oats & Cinnamon Start 15
Orange Creamsicle Delight 39

P
Peachy Keen Sunrise 16
Peanut Butter Jelly Time 33
Peppy Parsley Potion 72
Pineapple Parsley Pep 56
Protein Power-Up 77
Purple Berry Galaxy 37

R
Romaine Calm & Blend On 75

S
Simple Spinach Detox 54
Spinach Sunshine Sip 68
Spring Melon Medley 23
Strawberry Banana Smile 32
Summer Berry Splash 24
Sweet Spinach Stamina 83

T
Tangy Orange Daybreak 19
Tangy Raspberry Refresh 45
Tropical Mango Rapture 28
Tropical Refuel Shake 82
Tropical Treasure Hunt 36

W
Watermelon Basil Bliss 57
Winter Citrus Zest Fondue 26

Printed in Great Britain
by Amazon